IT'S MY TIME!

"Slow" Daughter Beats Older Siblings

IT'S MY TIME!

"Slow" Daughter Beats Older Siblings

Sadie Marie Carpenter
with
Duane L. Herrmann

Buffalo Press
Topeka, Kansas

Copyright © 2018 Duane L. Herrmann

All rights reserved. No part of this publication, or parts thereof, may be reproduced in any form, except for the inclusion of brief excerpts in a review without written permission of the publisher.

ISBN: 978-1-879448-12-4

Buffalo Press
Topeka, Kansas

IT'S MY TIME!
"Slow" Daughter Beats Older Siblings

Contents

Forward	3
Dead Lice Falling	4
My Entrance	6
Moving House	7
Drowning, or…	9
You Custard!	10
My Role in the Family	13
It's on This Eighty Acres	18
Easter	20
Farm Life	23
Christmas Gift	36
I Hate Winter	38
Home Life	40
Singing Career	57
Careers Teaching School	58
Attending School	61
Chick Mate	71
School Games	76
Reading	78
First Train Trip	85
My First Dress	87
Food Preparation	91
4-H Experience	94

Being Sick	100
Daddy's Stroke	102
Ridgecrest	104
My College Career	107
Family Reunions	116
Church	119
Nursery Maid	120
Grandpa Yoho	124
Mom	127
Genealogy	134
Epilogue	142

Forward

All through my childhood I had been told I was "slow," I was just not very smart. This was ground into my consciousness over and over and over, and in so many different, and not at all subtle, ways. Only as an adult, not so many decades ago, did I accidentally learn I was dyslexic. I was not slow, I was not dumb, my brain merely processed information in a different way than most other people perceive as "normal." Often, dyslexics are smarter than the people around them and think faster. Our brains are processing MORE information than other people deal with. And dyslexics are more creative and inventive than others.

"Where did you get that weird idea?" I am often asked. I don't know. Ideas just come.

This discovery of being dyslexic burst open such a dam of relief and amazement that I cried for days. My whole life suddenly made sense. I had tried so hard for so long, and nothing seemed to work. The knowledge of what dyslexia is, and how it affects the workings of the brain, made sense of all I'd experienced. It is no exaggeration to say this was a revelation. My understanding exploded, and my relief followed. The more I studied and learned, the more excited I became.

In their ignorance, the people around me had lied to me all my life! I had tried so hard, and my efforts had so often failed. I felt worthless. No one needs to suffer like that, so I'm offering this, the story of my own experience. I've already helped a nephew and his son;

both discovered they were dyslexic and, as often happens, both also have ADD.

I want more people to know what it is like to be dyslexic because too many others have been, and still are, treated the same way I was for the same reason, and don't know it. Society is most often not kind to those who are seen as "different." And dyslexics are "different." I want other people who are different to know they are not alone, we are not alone, and our difference is not bad. There is hope.

We dyslexics are intelligent people, often highly intelligent. We are creative and inventive. We are exceptional and that is important!!!

The following memoirs are not in chronological order, but more in subject order yet, since many aspects of life intertwine, where one subject ends and another begins is, at times, an arbitrary decision. And many aspects of life overlap, so expect some of that also. I hope that by sharing my experience of dyslexia, someone else may be able to avoid the negativity that was so much a part of my life.

My mother often told me, as a child, that one day my turn (for whatever) would come. Well, my time has finally arrived! This is my time to tell my story.

Dead Lice Falling

"You move like the dead lice were falling off you!" My mother screamed at me. This was one of her favorite ways to address me. When I tried to do an adult task she demanded I do, and failed since I was a child, she would add in exasperation, "You take two steps backward for every step forward!"

One time after she said the latter I glared as I stood in front of her and defiantly took one deliberate step forward, then two back. She simply stared at me, not comprehending I was literally fulfilling her expression. Then she ordered me to stop wasting time and do the work.

This encapsulates my childhood.

Though I was the fifth child out of six, with three older brothers and an older sister, who could have done the work more capably than myself, I was chosen to be the family workhorse. Among other things, I had to wash, dry and put away the dishes after meals, sweep and mop the floors, feed the chickens and gather their eggs (which were not easily located in nesting boxes, but scattered all through the chicken house and yard wherever the chickens decided to lay them), hoe weeds in the garden and fetch buckets of water. We had no water piped into the house, but that story comes later.

If there happened to be a party some evening which I wanted to attend, I could not. I had to stay home and work.

"Your turn's coming," or, "there will be other times," is what she would invariably say. My turn never came, nor were there other times as long as I lived at home. Is there any wonder that I wanted to get away? The isolation of our farm in the country was difficult enough, but to not be allowed to go to even the few events I knew about, was unbearable.

This even applied to church, though not to Sunday mornings. Our church also had a Sunday evening service. Daddy would attend these, and I wanted to go – every week! Mom could not actually refuse that, but she always found some task she insisted I must complete Sunday afternoon before I could go. No one else in the family was forced to work on Sundays – just me.

My Entrance

"It was a dark and stormy night..." Well, I'm really not sure. It was summer time, June 24, 1939, when I came into this world. Mom almost died. I was born at home and I had a twin who had died sometime during the pregnancy, but no one knew that then. After my birth, and the doctor had left thinking everything was fine, Mom began to hemorrhage. Daddy called the doctor and he was told to knead her stomach like a loaf of bread. He was desperate. What would he do with five young children, one a new baby, and no mother!! He couldn't lose his wife! He worked hard! This kneading action caused her uterus to expel the unborn, unknown fetus, as well as the placenta. It worked and she lived to be 89 years old.

The fetus, I was later told, had deteriorated to such condition that its gender could not be determined. No one ever hid the fact that I was a twin, and I missed her. I say "her" because I always felt as if we were identical girl twins. When my little sister, June, was born, I adopted her as my "twin." She didn't know any better. We became inseparable.

It's only been recently that I have become aware that I was a buffer between her and our mother. I was yelled at, not June. Being older, I was expected to do more work, and at an earlier age, than she was. I was also able to nurture and encourage her in ways I never experienced. I'm sure that my role allowed her to have the most nearly "normal" childhood of anyone in the family. Reasons for that will become readily apparent.

I do, though, still wonder what my life might have been like if my twin had survived. Her existence could have changed everything!

Moving House

I was born in the house my parents owned in the small community of Kaw Valley northeast of Topeka, Kansas. I was the last one of my family to be born there. My parents had settled there because my father had come to Topeka to attend Strickland's Business College. All the rest of his siblings were farmers or manual laborers and he wanted to do something different. He moved from Wilsey, Kansas to do this. By this time all his siblings were established in their own lives, so his parents followed him to Topeka.

Because he was the youngest in the family, with no family of his own yet, he signed a contract with his parents that he would take care of them in their old age and, in return, he would gain ownership of the few acres they bought in Kaw Valley. This property had only one house, so in preparation for his marriage, he and his brothers built him a small house close to that of his parents on that acreage. I was born in the big house. It no longer exists.

After my father's parents had died, my parents could not decide what to do with the second house, so it remained empty. One day, while my mother was washing dishes, and looking out the kitchen window to the other house, she impulsively decided to go to the other house. She carried the dishpan, full of soapy water and dirty dishes, to the other house. She set it down in the kitchen of the other house and finished washing the dishes there. As the children came looking for her, she instructed them to bring more things from the other house. When my father came home from work that night, he found his home dark and empty of his family. Looking around, he saw light from the other, supposedly empty, house. He walked over and found his family sitting down to dinner! Later, he and the children moved the rest of their furniture and belongings. This moving from one house to the other happened several times.

My mother didn't think anything was odd about this moving back and forth. Doing so gave her some element of control when most of her life she had had no control due to circumstances and social expectations forced on her. The simple decision to move to the other house cost nothing. Most of the effort of the move was done by others. The houses were side by side, so the effort of moving was minor. There were no utilities to transfer, because there were no utilities TO transfer (no running water, no garbage collection, no cable, and just one electric bill for both places). The garden, chickens and other livestock didn't need to be moved. The children's school was just a block away, no change there. The move was easy. The decision gave Mom power and a little variety in her life.

Eventually, after both of Daddy's parents died, he and Mom sold these two houses and the five acres they were on. One reason given for the move was that Mom didn't want to see another tub of diapers being washed away. She retained a graphic memory of that. With a constant stream of babies the loss of their diapers was devastating. The land the houses sat on was low enough, and next to a tributary of the Kansas River, that it would flood. Eventually, after the flood of 1951, the big house, closest to the creek, was taken down to make way for the flood control levee to protect Topeka.

Later in life, my mother moved house again, only she had to buy a neighboring farm first to do so. After the move, she walked around this "new" house as tickled as a little girl. The other farm was not sold and, some years later, she moved back to that house! You could almost say that moving from house to house was a life-long hobby of hers.

Drowning, or…

One summer day Daddy took my brothers and me swimming in the pool at Gage Park in Topeka. Mom never went swimming. I think she had nearly drowned one time, so she avoided large bodies of water. I was about two years old. Some people don't think a person can remember events that young, but if the event is sufficiently unusual, it can be remembered. This event was that unusual.

The park in those days had a big swimming pool. In the middle of the pool was an island you could swim to. Daddy took me to the island. I don't remember how, but for him to carry me was not unusual, so he probably did that. I don't remember. I just remember we were there, surrounded by water, and that was unusual. While we were sitting on the island my brother Jim, who was three years older than me, so he was about five or six years old, began to pester Stanley who was about ten. Stanley didn't want to put up with this, so he pushed Jim into the water. As Jim began falling, he reached for support – and grabbed me! We both went tumbling into the water together. THAT was unusual!!

I managed to hold my breath, but that's all I could do. I remember wondering, 'how was I going to get out of the water?' I kept my eyes open though. Everything looked strange down there, underwater. That, too, was shockingly unusual. Daddy reacted quickly and pulled me out and I was fine. I don't know what happened to Jim but he's still around, so he must have gotten out of the water too.

You Custard!

"Go back, you Custard!" Byron, the neighbor boy yelled at me. He didn't want me to play in his barn with my older brother and sister, Don and Juanita. In a corner of their barn was a stack of hay they were going to climb. It was a wet day and we were bored at home so we walked next door to his place. We didn't mind a little rain. He and I were the same age, six years old. What right did he have to tell me I couldn't come? And, why did he call me, "custard?" It sounded bad. It hurt to be called that bad sounding word. What was a custard? It didn't sound nice, and he didn't say it in a nice way, with that snarl in his voice. But I didn't know.

Later, when I was sitting on the ground beside Grandpa, helping him shell corn off the cob for chicken feed, I decided to ask him what the word meant. He was a grown-up, he ought to know. His reaction took me by surprise.

"Grandpa, Byron Myers called me a Custard…"

Grandpa laughed so hard he fell to his side and rolled on the ground. I couldn't even finish my question. What did the word mean? He didn't say. I didn't think it was funny. The word still hurt. Byron had said it in a mean way, it had to be bad. Why was Grandpa laughing at this bad word? I was very confused. He didn't tell me what the word meant.

That evening at supper, as we all sat at the table, grandpa repeated my question to the entire family. Everyone looked at me and laughed without restraint. I was embarrassed and confused. The boy had called me an obviously bad word, why were they laughing? And, what did it mean? I did not understand.

Later, my older brother told me to simply call the boy a custard in return. Though I still did not understand this bad word, his advice sounded reasonable to me.

The next time I saw Byron, with great satisfaction, I called him a custard.

"What did she say?" He asked my brother, puzzled. Apparently, he had forgotten.

Still, no one ever told me what the word meant. Only decades later did I realize he had a lisp and might well have been trying to call me a, "bastard," but was not familiar enough with the word to pronounce it correctly, though he did understand it did not have a good meaning.

Thinking about this later, another question arose: Where did he hear the word, yet not learn it enough to pronounce it correctly? Knowing his parents, it was not a word either of them were likely to have used. Could he have heard it, at school from another child? Or, from someone his father might have hired to help with work on their farm? I don't know. I never thought to ask him.

I eventually learned that a custard is a kind of food, and I learned to make it. Custard pie became my favorite, and it still is.

What a strange relationship with a word!

This same boy, who was our closest neighbor, was once given a little, toy dog. I asked him if I could see it. He didn't answer, but grabbed my arm and twisted it painfully. I don't know why he was so angry about it but my revenge eventually came.

One summer a few years later, the boy's mother, asked me if I would pick some gooseberries for her.

"Sure," I said. "How many do you want?"

"As many as you can pick," she answered.

She didn't know what she asked for, nor imagined how many I could pick. So, my sister, June and I (of course, she worked with me) went to the gooseberry patch. Gooseberries grow on a bush and are about the size of a pea. They hang from a stem and have a tail. The branches have thorns on them, so you very carefully lift the branch up and pick the berries.

Picking gooseberries is a lot like picking blackberries, only with gooseberries you have to take the stem and tail off each berry after it is picked. That's the hard part. We were not required to do that, she had only asked for them to be picked. Pulling off the stem was the part the Myers boys, Byron and Bruce, had to do. They were sure mad about their part of that job! They wanted to throw those gooseberries in the 'Boaz girl's' faces. I didn't care. It was get even time for me.

My Role in the Family

When I was two the family moved from the Kaw Valley community north of Topeka to a farm south of Tecumseh. We moved shortly after America entered World War II. I later learned that my mother and older sister, Juanita, were with a realtor looking at the farm on a nice Sunday afternoon in early December. No one would have remembered the date except for the news on the radio that the Japanese had just bombed some place in far off Hawaii they had never heard of. Now, no one can forget. The place was Pearl Harbor. The date was December 7, 1941.

They bought the farm and we moved. I don't remember any of that but I do remember another sunny December day two years later, when we were living on that farm. That morning my father came upstairs to my bedroom to get me up. He'd never done this before. I was four and a half years old. He told me to stay in bed until he came back to get me. He said Momma was sick and he had to get a bucket of water. I was to stay in bed and wait for him. I knew how long it took to go to the well and back for water, so I could be patient that long.

He came back a while later, got me dressed and took me downstairs. He took me into the kitchen where an uncle was washing dishes. That, also, had never happened before and I began to wonder what was going on. Being curious, I looked through a crack in the door.

Mom's bed was in the dining room on the other side of the dining table. There, on the table, was a baby. It was being washed. In a few minutes Daddy brought the baby to me and all I could think was, I had to act surprised. I didn't want to tell him I already knew about the baby. He said her name was June. I loved her immediately and we've been close ever since.

For some reason our mother decided that June was the smart child, but not pretty, and I was the less intelligent, but pretty child. She constantly made comments to reinforce these opinions. Others members of the family heard them and believed her. There was no evidence for any of these "facts."

The summer I was six years old, just before begin-ning school in the fall, my brother Jim, three years older than me, told me he would teach me my ABC's. I wondered at this uncharacteristic generosity.

"Oh, you're too dumb to learn," he said even before we began. I was too surprised to respond, then he walked off.

What was I to think? He was older, he knew more than I did, I believed him. I didn't know it wasn't true. Where did he get the idea? Had mom started saying it already? She said it often after I had started school, but before?

That fall, after being in school a while, one room with all eight grades, and starting to learn to read, I thought, 'He said I couldn't learn, but I am.' I had found a process that helped me learn. When I was reading the story in my reader and I came to a new word, I would go to the teacher and ask her to pronounce the word for me, then I would repeat it until I knew the word. I was a slow reader, but the more words I learned to read, the more I could read.

It didn't matter who the teacher was, they would always tell me the word I asked about. I appreciated their kindness and helpfulness. I never got that response at home. Despite my mother being a teacher, she wouldn't tell me such a simple thing as how to pronounce a word. After a few repetitions of each word, and using it in sentences, I knew it and I went on to another word. I didn't know my difficulty was due to dyslexia. If I hadn't had enough confidence, and trust, to ask the teacher how to pronounce words, I doubt that I would ever have learned to read. Many people with dyslexia don't learn to read. They struggle their entire lives.

I had believed my mother's comments about my slow and limited intelligence were accurate. Yet, my grades in school did not bear them out. Even the year I was in eighth grade, when my mother was my teacher and graded my papers, she could not acknowledge the inaccuracy of her negative opinions. Only a partial report card survives from that year. It shows the first four, not all six, grading periods. In those four periods of the year, she wrote: three As and a B in Social Studies; three Bs and a C in reading; four Bs in writing; three Bs and a C in spelling; one A, one B and two Cs in English; three Cs and a B in arithmetic; three Bs and a C in science; and four Bs in health. These were not the highest grades, but certainly not the grades of a "slow" learner, yet my mother continued to refer to me in those terms. She did promote me to ninth grade, so I must not have been that "slow!"

Unfortunately others in the family, as well as myself, began to believe this negative opinion of myself too! After years of hearing our mother's judgmental phrases referring to me as, "slow," and that I, "moved like dead lice were falling off" me, and I would, "take two steps back for every step forward," how could we not believe it? No alternative statements were ever made. Nothing positive or supportive was ever said. When all you hear about yourself is negative, you eventually begin to believe the negativity. And, when it is your mother, the authority in the house, who passes judgment on all things, how could it not be true? Mothers don't lie. Well – yes, they can! All because I was dyslexic!

As an adult, I eventually realized, **none** of it was true. Still, high school was harder than elementary school.

My grade school was a tiny country school of maybe twenty students in all eight grades in one room. The high school was huge in comparison, with 500 students, most who lived closer to town than I did, so as far as I was concerned they were all "city kids." I truly felt like the proverbial country bumpkin. That is not made up. It sounds trite, but it's accurate.

I had always liked school, it was more pleasant than being home. I wanted to learn, but didn't know how to study. Basically, in spite of my delight in being in school, the experience was painful. I couldn't spell, so taking a test was always difficult. No one seemed to care. Still, I didn't give up or drop out, and graduated with the rest of my class. Mom didn't seem to notice.

Years later my sister, June, mentioned her difficulties with geometry in high school and how, eventually, she needed a tutor's help to pass the class. I was stunned. I had been told by my mother to take algebra, with no preparation, and I flunked. No one suggested getting a tutor for me! Who suggested she have a tutor? And, why didn't anyone care that much about my struggles? She was "smart," so she deserved help? And, I was "slow," so I didn't deserve help? That is simply backwards! But, that is how our family treated the two of us.

I was once asked if I felt all of us, together, were a "family," or simply eight people who lived together.

We were just eight people who had to live together until we could get away. The boys were able to do that at a younger age than the girls. There were less choices for us girls.

It's On This Eighty Acres

Mom was not conscious about things. She would put things down wherever it might be convenient, then forget about them. This generated a similarly casual attitude in the rest of us. Neither she, nor anyone else, paid much attention where things were put. There was no specific "away" when we put things away. They were just put. Unless she had just had an item, asking her where something might be found was most likely futile.

"It's on this eighty acres," was her common response to the question about the location of some item. It was not helpful. It did not matter if the person was her husband, her child or a grandchild. "It's on this eighty acres," was, her stock reply when anyone wanted to know the location of anything. How she kept track of any important papers still remains a mystery to me.

If she did happen to know where something might likely be, and she wanted to, she could tell you, but that was rare. You couldn't count on it. She was just as likely to deliberately not tell you where something was, if that was her mood. Needless to say, this did not contribute to domestic bliss. Trying to find anything was an exercise in exasperation! Even if it was something important, the response was the same.

One day, later in life, her glasses went missing. This was not unusual. She needed them for reading, but found them a nuisance the rest of the time. When she finished reading, she would take them off, set them down – and forget about them. When she needed them again to read something, there was always a search for her glasses. After all of us children had left home, there was no one to help her look for them, except Daddy if he happened to be home.

She had searched for hours for her glasses and had begun to get seriously concerned. She had never before had such trouble in finding them. How could she have lost them so thoroughly?

Late in the day a grandson came to visit. He was familiar with the hopelessness of relying on her to know where something might be found, her non-committal, "it's on this eighty acres," and the frequent misplacement of her glasses. When she began to explain how this time her glasses were so totally lost, she had looked absolutely everywhere in the house and could not find them, he was not surprised. Then he noticed the problem.

"Granma," he said as he pointed up to her head. "They're in your hair!"

She felt the top of her head – and there were her glasses, indeed! The only place she couldn't see them while she looked! Her statement was true – her glasses **were** on those eighty acres! She enjoyed the joke!

Easter

For my family, Easter was always special. It was on an Easter day, March 31, 1929, that my family began. On Easter Sunday that year my parents went to church in Oklahoma City and, after Sunday School and before the church service, were married there. Many details of the event are now lost, for instance: why Oklahoma City? Neither of them lived there. It may have been that Oklahoma City was the "big town," to add to the adventure of getting married. Being away from the community where she was teaching, no one there would know because, at that time, married women were not allowed to teach. And, there were hotels there where they could spend their first married night.

Being married in Oklahoma made sense because she lived and taught in Oklahoma. Dad, being an employee of the railroad, could ride the train there for free. Oklahoma City could have been the logical meeting place. She went back to her school the next day and finished teaching the rest of the semester, which she said ended in April, before she moved to Kansas. We don't know where she was teaching that year, but it must have been close to the city for her to have been able to get there and back on the train in the short time available. When school was out, at the end of that semester, she moved to Topeka and became a housewife.

They had met on a train when mom was traveling from Oklahoma to see her mother's relatives in Holton, Kansas. He rode the train from Topeka to visit his brother in Wichita. The seat beside her was empty and he asked to sit there. She picked up her hat in the seat and he sat down. The relationship began.

One Saturday, the day before Easter, Mom went to town while I stayed home and cleaned house. I mopped the floor, ironed, and did whatever else she had said needed to be done. When Mom came home, she had gotten June a new dress, hat and shoes. For me, there was only a pair of socks. The unfairness of that made me mad. I needed more than that!

Many years later, but on another Easter, Mom and Daddy and I were in town the Saturday before. I wanted a new dress and knew the only way to have one was to make it. I was used to that, I just needed the fabric. It took some effort to convince Daddy to spend the money. The cost was less than $5.00, but he didn't want to spend it. I finally convinced him. When we got home I spent the rest of that day and evening making the new dress. I finished it and wore it to church that Sunday morning. It wasn't the last time I entirely made a dress on Saturday to wear to church the next day. It's now my turn not to have to do that anymore in order to have clothes to wear!

Daddy made Easter special for us kids too. My older brother Don remembers the first time Daddy did that. It was some time before I was born. The first "Easter eggs" consisted of a dishpan full of jelly beans. The eggs eventually became a specific special egg for each child. It was a large chocolate egg with our name on it. Dad would hide the eggs and each of us had to find our own. If we found someone else's egg, we could not tell them where we had found it. We had to look until we found our specific egg!

Most of the time these eggs were chocolate and hollow. Some years the eggs were solid candy. All the eggs were decorated with flowers, and other seasonal decorations: bunnies, small eggs, etc. Each egg was in a protective box with a see-through lid so you could read the name which had been written with frosting.

As grandchildren were born, eggs for them were also added. No one went without an egg. Even a new-born baby had its own egg. Eventually there were dozens of eggs, each to its own hiding place, different each year. Daddy delighted in finding these hiding places and, since ours was not the smallest farmstead, there were several buildings and LOTS of hiding spaces. Some of these hiding places included unmounted tires in a barn, behind a bale of hay leaning at an odd angle (he made many of these spaces while he hid the eggs), an upturned bucket, a plastic bag caught in the weeds, the remains of a rain-soaked cardboard box, and under large broken chunks of cement dumped to fill and raise up the driveway. It could take hours to find your egg! All the while he was tickled with the attention.

Some years even cousins of grandchildren were included in the egg hunt. Daddy invited them when the number of grandkids who could come was small. He liked watching the hunting. Once, when my children and I returned to Topeka to visit, and my daughter could participate, she wondered how Grandpa knew how many eggs to buy and the names of all the children. Many of whom she didn't know. The Easter egg hunt was our major family event.

Farm Life

At the end of 1941, my parents purchased a farm of eighty acres on Tecumseh Rd, east of Topeka, half a mile north of 45th street. The house had no electricity or plumbing; that was not unusual in those days. The house we left did have electricity, and maybe plumbing, I was too young to remember such a detail. Electric wires were expected to reach the house soon, so no one thought that would be a problem.

Shortly after we moved to the farm America began to gear up to fight in World War II. Not long after that, all electric utilities in the country were ordered to halt the extension of their power lines to homes. They were not considered essential for the war effort. The lines would not reach our house. My mother took it hard: she was devastated. I'm sure this contributed to her depression.

She had expected to have electricity as she had at our old place, now no one knew how long it would take to reach the house. It was the only time I ever saw her cry. I was so young, I had no idea how much of a difference electricity would make in our lives; washing clothes, ironing, even lighting. She knew. In the next several years, I learned.

Power lines finally reached us when I was in the fourth grade. It changed our lives, it changed my life! More about that later. Indoor plumbing took longer, much longer.

This new house was not really very large, but was a typical farmhouse for the time it was built. Downstairs were three rooms: kitchen, living room and another room that we used at times as a dining room or a bedroom – sometimes both. Upstairs there were two rooms. Daddy divided the largest into two small bedrooms, one for him and Mom, the other for Juanita and me, and June when she came along. The three of us had one double bed. There was barely room to walk around three sides of it. My three brothers and Grandpa, in the summer time when he lived with us, all shared the largest bedroom. It had two double beds. Under the house was a dark and damp, low-ceilinged basement with a dirt floor.

We didn't use the basement much except to store the food we canned. The dirt floor prevented other uses. Eventually, after I had left home and the house was expanded, a cement floor was put in the basement, but it was still not used much. Originally, inside steps went down to the basement from the kitchen. In the remodel those steps were removed and that space was used for a tiny, inside bathroom. The bathtub was tucked under the steps going upstairs. The only steps from then on were from the back porch which had been enclosed in the remodeling. There had been outside steps there all along. In the remodeling, cement was simply poured over them to make new steps. The low ceiling of the basement and the new steps on top of the old ones, meant that the top of the basement door was, for most people, about chest high. You had to stoop down to get in or out of the basement. Of course, no one did that if they could avoid it! It was a usable, unusable basement! Typical of my family's (lack of) planning!

Originally, there were three exterior doors to the house, one on the west, the side to the road, opening to the living room, the apparent "front" of the house, which was seldom used. There was one on the south, closest to the driveway, opening to the dining room/bedroom, which was sometimes used. And, one on the east, opening to the kitchen, which was the one most used as it gave the most direct access to the outbuildings: the barn, chicken house and, most significantly, the outhouse. Here was also the porch, an extra room-like space, used for all kinds of reasons, but mostly miscellaneous, storage. It was not enclosed, that came later.

There were several significant outbuildings. Already mentioned were the outhouse, barn, and chicken house, of which there were two, a big and little one, plus a corn crib and shed for implements. The well, our source of water was outside too – past the barn and down the hill a ways. It was becoming known that wells should not be downhill from barnyards and all the animal waste, but ours was. Daddy took a sample of the water to be tested and it came back, "safe for human consumption," but I still wonder. I don't know about my siblings, but as a child I was sick a lot. As adults, though, we have seldom been sick. Maybe the "unhealthy" location of the well built up our immunity and wasn't so bad for us after all!

You could say we had running water, but it was usually one of the children who did the running! When the water bucket became empty, one of us was ordered to, "run get a bucket of water." Often that order was directed toward myself. It was easier for my older siblings, but that didn't matter. All I can remember is that two-gallon bucket, filled with slopping water, felt like it weighed a ton! And, I would get wet in the process. That didn't matter. If the bucket wasn't full enough to my mother's satisfaction, she would yell at me. If it was full enough, it was too full for me to carry all that distance without splashing. When the path was wet muddy or icy, getting water was a horrible, even dangerous, task.

Despite the distance from the house, past the barn into the pasture several hundred yards and down a gully, the hardest part was negotiating the well itself. The sides of the well rose a couple feet or so above the ground. One had to climb up to the top which was covered with wooden planks. The rocks arranged as steps up the side were haphazard at best. It was not safe, especially not when wet, either from rain or after water had been splashed from pumping and trying to move the bucket. Iced over in the winter, it was absolutely treacherous! But, that's just the way it was. We were warned to be careful, so if we slipped and fell, it was our own fault! I hated it.

I don't know why the sides of the well were so high above the ground. Now that I think of it, the height was probably to ensure that no cow would walk over the well and get a foot caught in the planks or even fall in. I know the tops of the wells other people had, closer to their houses, where no animals would roam, were only a step above the ground. If ours had been, getting water would have been much easier! There was so much that was difficult for me, I just had to endure it. Oh, well.

The pump on top of the well was a typical hand pump. Electricity never reached that far, so an electric pump would have been usable. It stood taller than I was when I first had to get water. Gradually, as I grew, it became shorter and shorter. The pump had a nozzle where the water came out, and some pumps had a hook near the end of the nozzle to hang the bucket. The pump was muscle powered. It had a handle to be "pumped" up and down to bring the water up. A pipe inside the housing of the pump extended down into the water to bring the water up. That kind of pump was so common, I've never thought to describe it to anyone before.

After the bucket was as full as I could barely carry, there was the trek back to the house. After carefully climbing down the rock steps on the side of the well, there was the hill to climb with the full bucket. . Once that had been navigated, the walk to the house, despite the distance, was much less of a problem. The gate into the pasture where the well was located was another matter. Stop. Put the bucket down, open the gate, go through with the bucket, put the bucket down again to shut the gate, then on to the house. I almost forgot another "normal" part of this trek – to watch for, and avoid, the random cow droppings which could be anywhere in the pasture! Sometimes, it was an obstacle course!

Because the well was so far from the house, no one wanted to go there very often, and certainly, no one wanted to go there after dark! When we did get a bucket of water, we would use it sparingly! We learned early not to waste water. We used one two-gallon bucket of water a day for a family of six. That seems impossible now, but it was normal while I grew up. I use more water now, but I still don't waste any!

Now that we had a "real" farm of eighty acres, not just the measly five acres we had before, my father could be "a farmer." All five of his brothers were farmers and his five sisters had married farmers. He was the youngest and the only one with a city desk job. He likely took some kidding about his easy life and "work" that was not work, not "real" work anyway. Having a farm and farm animals was a way for him to be a farmer too. My father obtained a small tractor and implements to farm the cropland which we had as well as pasture. Maybe he thought the farm would give his boys some work to do. It did, but that was not very beneficial to them or the rest of us. June and I had to work in the fields too!

We had at least four cows to milk. We had all the milk we wanted to drink, and more cream than we could ever use. It rose to the top of the milk and had to be skimmed off. The cream we didn't use, we often would churn into butter. That was a long, exhausting and tedious process – just the task for a little girl to be given, and I was the little girl! June did some too, eventually, but never as much as her big sister.

During World War II, for some reason, we got the new-fangled margarine. It was white and tasteless. At the time, we didn't know it had no nutritional value, and was actually harmful; it was just new – and exciting. It came in clear plastic bags. It was exciting because yellow coloring came in an orange bead in the bag of white stuff. To make it look like butter, you had to knead the bag with your hands. The heat from your hands, and the motion, gradually dissolved the coloring and it all became yellow. That was a fascinating and mysterious process. June and I were both eager to squeeze the margarine and watch the color change. It was the most exciting thing we could do!

The cows added to Daddy's work considerably. Every morning before going to his town job, and every evening after coming home, he had to feed and water and milk the cows. The cows produced far more milk than our family could use. The excess milk had to be taken care of until it could be hauled away by the dairy to process to make into cheese. This was supposed to be income for the family, but somehow, brother Jim always managed to pull the payment check out of the mail before anyone else saw it, and he avoided as much work as he could!

A time or two, June and I tried to use the cows for entertainment. There was little other entertainment, we had to find what we could. The cows were there, in the pasture, we tried to make use of one of them. Somehow, we managed to get on the back of a cow and tried to ride it like a horse. The cow would have none of it. It just stood there and did not move! So much for being cowgirls!!

Daddy never owned a bull. That would not have been safe for us. Bulls are territorial and we had only one pasture – the one we had to walk through to get to the well. There was no way a bull would tolerate that! So, a bull was brought in every year to, euphemistically, "freshen" the cows. Cows only produce milk after having a calf, so impregnating a cow was a regular process. We never kept the calves after they were born. I don't know what happened to them. I suppose us children weren't told. They were born, then simply disappeared.

One summer day, when I was three, Daddy was in the barn milking the cows. I was there with my brother Donny. Daddy wanted the cow to move, so he kicked the cow. Unexpectedly, in response, the cow kicked Daddy and broke his leg. Mom put Daddy in the car to take him to the hospital. Of course, I wanted to go too. "Hospital" sounded like an exciting place, but then, any trip in the car was exciting. Mom didn't need a three year old going along so, thinking quickly, she said I would have to have a bath first. My older sister, Juanita, was told to bathe me.

We had no bathtub, or bathroom, so, as usual, she had me stand on the kitchen table while she washed me. From that height I saw Mom drive out of the driveway without me. I was dismayed. There went my trip to the special hospital place! In time, Daddy's leg healed and he was up and around again.

One day Daddy came home with some baby quail in a box which he wanted to use to stock the farm. He said he was going to put them on a certain big rock by the creek. He let me come with him when he carried the quail there. I was old enough to know that baby chickens required our careful care and attention. The quail were like little, baby chicks and would need care too. No one could be out in the pasture to care for the quail so I worried about them. He repeatedly told me they would be fine on their own. I couldn't believe him.

There was a big flat rock by the creek that he put the quail on. He put some chicken feed out for them and we left. I don't know what happened to the quail and I don't know why we didn't keep them at the house until they got bigger and more able to take care of themselves. I never saw them again. Their fate became one of the many things I never knew. A lot of things were not explained to me.

Every spring, June and I would start looking for baby kittens. We would watch the momma cat as she got fatter and fatter. Suddenly, she would be thinner and we knew she had had her kittens. We would begin to look in the barn until we found them. They were the most exciting things we looked for! Holding a tiny, baby kitten, especially before it could open its eyes, was a special kind of treat. If their eyes were opened by the time we found them, we considered ourselves "late." After we found the kittens we would check to see which was a boy or girl. We could tell the difference and felt competent in knowing.

Some years Mom would order baby chickens for us to raise into hens. This was part of her effort to earn money. We sold the eggs which the grown chickens produced and we sold some of the chickens as "fryers," for people to cook. And, guess who got to prepare those?

When the baby chicks came, in special boxes in the mail, she would put newspaper on the floor in one corner of the living room. Then she would take some boards to make a square. She would put the baby chicks down on the floor in this corner. They lived there for a while. Days or weeks later she would put them in the small chicken house and keep them there until they were big enough to put in the big chicken house. As they grew, they needed more space and cleaning up after them became more and more work.

Nowadays, chickens are STILL shipped in special boxes through the post office! I was amazed when I recently learned that. It's something I hadn't thought of for decades! At least once, decades before I was born, a child about two years old, was sent to relatives through the post office. Soon, regulations were drawn up to prevent that. Who would have thought?

Baby chickens are very cute, and fascinating when the are little, but they do grow up after a few months. Some of the grown chickens would be kept to lay eggs and others were killed and dressed for eating. That was a big job for two small kids because it was up to June and me to do the work. When you are eleven years old, you just want to play. For some reason my mother had decided that I had to be working at all times. I was never thanked or paid for the work I did. And, since I was young, my objections didn't matter. I guess she was tired of taking care of the family and decided I could do as much of it as possible. I fervently hoped a time would come when I wouldn't have to do so much work – and that time has finally come!

For butchering and cleaning the chickens, we would have to get a bucket of water from the well which was heated in the tea kettle on the kitchen stove until it was just the right temperature, near scalding hot. One of us would hold the chicken while the other chopped its head off with an ax. I'm still amazed to this day that we both have all ten fingers to this day.

Next we would put the headless chicken in the scalding hot water for a short length of time. This enabled us to pull off the feathers. Pulling feathers was a tedious task. The wet, loose feathers would stick to your fingers, then you couldn't grip the next feathers to pull them. And, even after the feathers were off, there was often some root left in the skin and this had to be worked out with pressure on both sides of the pore the feather had grown from. Talk about gross!

With the feathers off, we could then take the chicken into the house to singe it over the fire of the stove, quickly burning off the last bits of hair-feathers too small to pull. Then we would wash the chicken carcass and cut it up, being careful while removing the guts. You did NOT want to puncture the guts!! The stuff inside the guts was smelly and messy. IF that stuff got out, it meant you had to be super careful in washing it all off, which might mean even another trip to the well for more water!

There was some excitement involved though, and that was finding eggs that had not yet been laid before the chicken had been killed. They would be in line, ready to be laid, largest to smallest. The largest one would have been the next to be laid. It would be full-size, or nearly so, with a soft shell. The shells of all these unlaid eggs were soft. You could poke them. That was fun. The smaller the eggs became, the more fascinating they were. We saved them to eat just like regular eggs – they were regular eggs, just in miniature. There was a certain size, I can't remember now, when the smaller eggs didn't have yokes. That was curious. The yoke was the food for the embryonic chicken. That was curious, too.

After the chicken was very clean, it could be cut into pieces (guess who got to do that too!) to be fried. All of this work was for just one meal. Our family was so large, one grown chicken would only make one meal. Next day we would have to do it all over again! But only in summer time or Saturdays when we were home.

Most children don't think of all that when they think of eating fried chicken. For us killing and cutting up the chicken was all part of the process of preparing the chicken to be fried.

In spite of all that work, those fried chicken dinners were good. However, there was a downside. We had to kill and clean several chickens each time. Mom didn't want to waste the hot water on only one chicken. And, if you're going to do one, you might as well do two or three. I disagreed, but I had no vote. We only ate one, Mom sold the rest. In addition to all the work, there was an additional downside. While we were killing and preparing the chickens, other girls were taking piano or dance lessons which we could not. I had always wanted to take piano lessons, all my older siblings had lessons, but not me.

The reason given was, there was no teacher. I don't know what happened to the teachers of the others, but no attempt was made to find a teacher for me. Was no effort made because I was considered not smart enough? I can only assume so. Later, my older sister found a piano teacher for June. I was glad for her, but it left me the only one out – and I had really wanted to learn! Some kids hated their music lessons, I wanted music lessons!

I especially remember the summer of the soy beans. I had turned 14 that summer, and June was nine and a half. The weeds had grown too big to get out any other way so it was up to June and me to hoe them out. All summer long, day after day it was: get out there and hoe. There were sixteen acres of them: row after long row, day after long, hot day. Mom would make us get up by five in the morning when it was still cool to go out and begin to hoe. It's an experience everyone should try for one eighteen hour day! Mom said Jim would hoe when he got home, but of course, he didn't. It was such a relief when school started and we could stop hoeing!

For all that work, Mom took June and me to town and bought us each two dresses. Our older brother, Jim, who was supposed to have worked with us, but did not, received a car. Really? Why? I never understood that – and still don't!

It was a short-lived relief, though, when school started. That year I would be going to high school. It proved to be another trying time.

Christmas Gift

One Christmas, not too long after we moved to the country and I was about three, we went to a program at the church that was just to the north of us about a mile. It was a small country church with a cemetery. The cemetery, Bethel Cemetery, is all that remains.

Our neighbors, the Myers family, with two boys, attended the church and most likely had invited us. The oldest of their boys was my age. Sometimes he and I were friends, sometimes not. It was his call more often than mine.

At the church he decided we were not friends. To emphasize this point he twisted my arm. Wrung it would be a better term. He grabbed my arm with both of his hands, close together, and twisted them in opposite directions. I was amazed the amount of pain that caused. It felt like he was pulling my skin apart. This experience is tied to what happened later.

We were given Christmas gifts. These gifts and their recipients were not well paired. I received something I'd never seen before. It looked like food, so I began to eat it. Just before I had a mouthful, my oldest brother stopped me. He told me not to eat it. It was not food, it was colored clay. He said he would show me what to do with it when we got home. And, he did.

He showed me how to make balls and ropes with the clay. That was about all I could do, but for me at that young age, it was amazing. I'd never encountered any substance like that before. There was such a large age difference between us that he did not often spend time with me. I remember this one special time when he did.

Was this my first Christmas gift? I can't remember, but very likely it was. I do remember that Christmas, generally, was not a major event in my family. I would often receive a doll, but that was about it. There were no Christmas parties and we didn't visit relatives. No one came to visit us. Oklahoma was too far for all of us to go see Aunt Reba, who we wanted to see; going there would have been an expedition. Any trip would have been an expedition, and we couldn't all fit into the same car anyway, so family trips were out, yet with Daddy employed by the railroad, we could ride the train for free. Why didn't we do that? I don't know. My family could have done so much more than we did. We barely kept going from day to day. Was that due to mom's depression? Probably so.

I don't remember any special meal at Christmas, and most years not even much of a tree, if there was one at all. There were no decorations. To say the house was rather drab, is an under-statement.

I Hate Winter

Winters were so cold and snowy. Mom always put up a blanket in the stairway, mid-way up, to keep the warm air from going upstairs. And it worked. The upstairs rooms stayed very cold. We would jump into bed as quickly as possible to conserve as much body heat as we could. We hated that blanket. In addition to blocking heat, it was always in the way going up or down. It's a wonder no one got caught in it and fell!

The only means we had to heat the house was a pot bellied, wood burning stove in the living room and a smaller wood cook stove in the kitchen. When the fire went out, which it did every day while everyone was gone, the house was cold, as cold as outside. When I was the first one to come home in the afternoon, the house would be freezing. It was sometimes colder inside than outside when the sun was shining. I could never get a fire started on my own. I would put wood in the stove and some paper just like grandpa, but it would never burn like it did for him. He did it so easily, but he always left to spend the winter in Oklahoma with Mom's sister, Aunt Reba. June wasn't any more successful starting a fire than I was. We had to wait in that freezing house
until someone else came home who could start a fire. It was sometimes so cold we could see our breath. Is it any wonder that I hate winter?

Of course, if the house was cold, the bed was cold. Going to bed in the winter was like sleeping on ice. The sheets felt frozen when you first got in. I HATE winter!

I knew not to complain. I was not allowed to complain about anything. When I tried to present my case, I was ridiculed or humiliated, often both, and learned to suffer in silence. Nothing was solved, but my silence avoided compounding the pain of my parent's response.

Even riding in the car was cold. It seemed to take forever for the heater to warm the inside of the car. Of course, the car was not as insulated and sealed as cars are today. And, as a child, I had to sit in the back seat. The house was cold, the car was cold, outside was cold. Is it any wonder I hate winter?

Another reason for hating winter was wearing long johns. We had to wear this long underwear in order to stay warm when we walked to school every day. Not only was that two mile walk cold, but the icy ruts and snow on the gravel roads were difficult to walk on. The school house wasn't evenly heated, the kids closer to the stove were warmer than those further from it, and guess where I had to sit? And, the playground was covered with ice and snow, so there wasn't much we could play outside. I hated being so cooped up!

As an adult, I learned about Seasonal Affective Disorder, and that there are many other people like me who, by mid-winter, just feel as if they're going to die! I'd thought I was the only one. I could handle the early half of winter, but as the days stay colder, in January and February, the clouds seem never to disburse. I felt it was never going to end. Those last few weeks of winter were the worst. Every winter, in January and February, I was sure I was going to die. Even the longer hours of sunlight don't help much. Only by mid March did I begin to feel a little better. Eventually, though, by May I was feeling better and could function for the rest of the year – until winter approached again, then the seasonal dread would set in. Awareness of this annual pattern doesn't lessen its impact. Is it any wonder I hate winter?

Now, I live in Arizona, the sun shines nearly every day, it's never so cold as in Kansas, and the winters aren't so bad. Now it IS my turn!

Home Life

My mother was a casual housekeeper and a generally negligent parent. She could not notice things until it became blatantly obvious, then she would scream that something be done about it immediately! The things that she would tolerate were odd. She told me of a time when I was about two and eating breakfast. It must have been oatmeal, or something similar. She noticed me eating while sitting on the floor. That didn't bother her. Our cat was beside me. I don't know how long it may have gone on, but she finally noticed that I was not simply eating – I was also feeding the cat! One spoonful for me, one spoonful for the cat; one spoonful for me, one spoonful for the cat!

How could a parent not notice, or care, that their child was eating on the floor – and feeding the cat alternate spoonfuls?? It is beyond me!

My father built us a swing set. He brought home some very long pipes, fifteen or twenty feet long; I don't know for sure, but they were very long. When it was finished it was the tallest swing set I'd ever known. I don't know how he made it by himself, and raised it into position, but he did.

It had three swings and a rope to climb. Because the pipes were so tall, you could swing way far out. It was breath-taking! To swing that high took a lot of effort, but the sensation of being weightless for those few moments at the top of the arc were worth the effort. And, on hot days, the wind blowing past your skin and through your hair cooled you off real fast!

The swing set was completed when I was about four or five. I watched my older brother, Don, and sister, Juanita, swing on this new thing, showing off to each other. They were enough older than I was that they had lots of experience swinging. I had not. They began to swing without using their hands. They didn't swing much, but I was impressed! They made it look so easy. After they left, I climbed on to one of the swings and, after swinging a bit, I also took my hands off like they had. I was not as experienced and had no balance. I flew out of the swing and landed on my face! I still remember the shock of falling and the bloody nose!

It wasn't a serious nose bleed and that experience didn't prevent me from swinging after that. The swing was our only play equipment and our major entertainment. Eventually, when the first seats broke, we learned to make replacements. We only needed pieces of wooden boards. We would hunt around in a shed for a board, and there always were some, and notch it to fit, then we could swing some more!

We didn't have a refrigerator for a long time; instead we had an ice box on the back porch. It was a bulky, insulated steel box about three feet tall and about five feet long. Food that needed to be kept cold was put in this box. Daddy would stop at the ice house on his way home from work and get a fifty pound block of ice. He would set the ice on the front bumper of the car, which extended a distance from the car, to carry it home. The ice would melt some to conform to the shape of the bumper, but amazingly, the ice would not melt significantly even though the trip took half an hour.

After the war we got electricity. What a wonder it was to turn on a light! To put away the oil lamps was a great relief. We no longer had to clean or fill them, or trim the wicks. With them, there was always a faint odor of kerosene in the house. Now, when we came home at night we could just flip a switch to turn on a light. The light was much brighter than the coal oil lamps, almost like daylight, even at night, and the house didn't smell. Life was a little better. Of course, dirt was more visible too, but that was minor.

Daddy also put a big pole light in the yard between the barn and the house. We didn't have to walk outside in the dark anymore. Now, going to the outhouse was so much easier, and safer, at night! Still, neither June nor I wanted to go there alone. Sometimes, one of us had to persuade the other that we urgently had to, "GO!"

To have been able to take a bath in a bathtub would have been pure delight, but that was not possible. There was no bathroom. Instead, to clean up, we had to heat a pan of water on the kitchen stove then take it up to our bedroom and wash ourselves. We called it, "a sponge bath," though we seldom had a sponge to use. We had a washrag, which really was a rag, some piece of old clothing, cut to a smaller size to use for washing things, us included. Mom didn't care what kind of rag it was: a rag was a rag was a rag.

Water was an entire endeavor all in itself. The house had no running water, no plumbing, no pipes. The water came from a well that was twice as far from the house as the barn, past the barn and down a slope, almost in a ravine. And, guess who had to go get the water!

There was a cistern near the house and, at one time rainwater from the roof was diverted to it. It would have been very nice if we could have used that water, but it was dirty and unfit to drink, and there wasn't much there. We couldn't even use that water to clean with, so a trip to the well in the pasture, about an eighth of a mile, was a daily necessity.

But the cistern could have been cleaned. The pipes supplying water to it from the gutters could have been maintained. And, if the cistern leaked, that could have been repaired. We could have had water right there by the house. Even if there was little rain, water could have been hauled in. Other people in the neighborhood did these things, why didn't my parents? I don't know. There was even a community well only a few miles away where we could have gotten water. Life could have been so much easier!

At the time, I didn't know these things, and had no voice in the family anyway. Something was seriously wrong. As a child, I had no clue. I just struggled through each day.

The two-gallon water bucket was placed on a stool in a corner of the kitchen with a dipper in it. When anyone, and I mean ANYONE, wanted a drink of water, they would go over to the bucket, fill the dipper and drink from that. That was common practice in most homes. We only used glasses to drink from at meal times. There were no disposable cups!

The one bucket of water had to last all day: for drinking, washing dishes and washing up at night. Major tasks, such as washing dishes or moping a floor, required nearly an entire bucket of water. Once those became my jobs, getting the water for them also became my job. Even though my older brothers and sister benefitted from my work, and I was much younger, they never got the water I needed. The boys would leave the house and Juanita would become engrossed in a magazine. June was too little: I was stuck. It's my turn now! I can simply turn a faucet – and there is all the water I need! Like magic!

Plumbing, and a bathroom, wasn't put in the house until after I left home for college. Once again, I was left out!

I can't understand, to this day, why, when both Mom and Daddy both worked, they didn't have the house remodeled and have running water sooner. I never got to enjoy the luxury of a bath in a bathtub until I'd left home! What an amazing joy it was!! So much water, and so easy to get! Simply turn the knob! Amazing!

When the electric lines reached the house, they were extended to the barn also. Daddy still milked cows, but now, in the winter time, he didn't have to do it in the dark with just a lantern to make a tiny circle of light.

We did have a telephone all the time though. The line had reached our house before the war. The phone was on the wall beside the south, outside door of the dining room. It was housed in a large wooden box, with a crank on the side to operate it. Of course, we were on a party line, which meant we could hear the phone ring for other houses on our line – all the phones rang at the same time, and if we wished, we could pick up the receiver and listen to the other conversations. It was considered rude, but sometimes we did. You could not make a call while anyone else on the line was using their phone. Phone calls were limited, a far cry from the personal cell phones which people, even children, have today!

When I was young, there was never enough food, sometimes not for meals at home, but definitely not to take to school for lunch. As a result, June and I would hide food at home when Mom bought groceries. It was for our own self survival. If we didn't hide it, our three bigger brothers would eat it all. Bananas became our favorite food to hide. They were special and easy to hide. If we got enough, we could have them for our lunch all week long. One day when Mom came home with a big bunch of bananas, June or I grabbed them and hid them. Our brother Don came in and wanted to where all the bananas were. He had seen them, but now couldn't find them. I didn't say a word – they were ours!

And, pears from the pear tree on the way to school was Free Food! Like manna from Heaven! If there were pears without spots or other blemishes, we would take them to school and trade with some other child for some of their lunch. Those were bonus lunch days! Any other food was more exciting than what little we had brought from home. We would often trade parts of our lunch at school. Even if what we brought to eat was not a balanced meal, after the trade it was more balanced.

There were times when June and I would cooperate to fix breakfast. This was usually during the summer, or on Saturdays. One of us would mix up batter and the other would fry the pancakes. It was an activity we enjoyed together. And, we cleaned up together too!

When June and I became bored, in those few times we weren't working, and we'd read all the books in the house, we'd go to the barn and find small boards easy to hold and go killing. We'd kill wood bees: Wack-a-Bee! They were big, buzzed loudly and didn't sting. There were lots of them and they were perfect targets! They were a challenge too, because they flew erratically. It took skill and luck to hit one that even flew low enough for us to reach. Chasing after them, and swinging at them, gave us lots of exercise. There were lots of these bees in the barn eating holes in the unpainted wood.

Their eating the wood is a cause of weakening old wooden buildings leading to their collapse.

When we tired of the bees we might go to the creek at the back of the farm almost a half mile from the house. We would play in the water until the number of leeches on our feet were a bother. We couldn't see the leeches in the water, but they could find us. These leeches were black and could be as long as an inch. When you tried to pull them off, if you held them at the end, they would stretch several times their normal size. To actually pull them off, they had to be grasped at the head where they had attached themselves to your body. After they were off they left a small round circle that would bleed. They attached themselves in order to suck blood. And to think, now, like two hundred years ago, doctors sometimes use them to remove blood from patients!

We had a cousin, Ina, who was the same age as my older sister, Juanita. When her mother, our father's sister, remarried, Ina came to live with us for three months while the newlyweds went to California. She would later stay with us from time to time because her stepfather was difficult to be around. She is sure he never liked her.

On one of these visits, while I was still very young, Juanita and Ina were instructed to clean and mop the kitchen floor. Mom had to leave the house and wanted it done while she was gone. Neither of the girls wanted to do it, and since I was younger than both of them, they decided I would be their labor force. Unfortunately for me, they could not agree on what I was to do. There was a stool in the kitchen that needed to be moved. Juanita wanted me to move it out of the way to one corner of the room, Ina insisted I move it to a different corner. Neither one would move it themselves. Soon, the two were engaged in a screaming match. I just stood there, not knowing what to do. Looking back on it now, I can see how ridiculous the whole situation was, but at the time I was utterly bewildered. I don't know if they ever got the floor clean!

Ironing clothes was a big job. Since we had no electricity in the house, we could not use an electric iron, we had to use flat irons. This was a piece of iron with a handle. It was set on the stove to heat up to just the right temperature. If it was too hot it would burn the garment, and of course, you didn't want that.

I began ironing at the ripe old age of about six or seven. It seemed like it was very easy to burn myself. The iron was set on the stove to get hot and when it got cool I would have to set it on the stove again.

When we got electricity the flatirons went out the door, though some people kept them for doorstops! More and more it became my job to iron. It didn't take long before I was doing all the ironing. I had three brothers and a father who wore shirts that they all wanted ironed. If you do the math, that's a lot of ironing in a week! Where was Mom? I don't know; I was just trying to get the ironing done. Maybe she was in bed where she spent a lot of her time. After a while I decided everyone else could iron their own clothes, I was tired of doing it. And that was that! Amazingly, no one insisted that I continue.

We had one board game that June and I would sometimes play. It was our only toy. It was called a "Puker Board." The game is still played, but it has a different name now. It is somewhat like Sorry. There were partial holes half the size of a marble to hold marbles. The holes formed a square near the outside of the board. In addition, each side of the board had four "holes" as the home base for each player's marbles. Each player had four marbles of the same color.

The game started with all the marbles at "home" and each player rolled a die hoping to get a six or one to enable one to begin. Once a marble was in play, any number of the die would allow the marble to be moved that many spaces. One time, while we tried to play the game, Jim began to pester June and me so much that we could not play. Mom was there and became so angry at him that she grabbed the board and hit him over the shoulder with it – and broke the board! That ended the game! Later, the uncle who had made the board for us made a second one.

Another time, Jim was pestering me so much, in desperation, I picked up the closest thing available – and threw it at him. It was a 2x4 piece of lumber, over a foot long. I missed.

I remember the one time Daddy played with June and me. He had gotten the measles and could not go to work for at least two weeks. He seldom got out of bed. The second week, as he was feeling better, he would get up for part of the day, but he knew he couldn't be up for very long or do any work, so he did not get dressed. One afternoon, while wearing his bathrobe, he came outside to play ball with June and me. In the yard! In his bathrobe!! Playing!!! This was astonishing and unforgettable!

I remember that sometimes, if we wanted play money, June and I would make our own. We would start with a real coin and use it as a pattern for a circle. We drew the circles on cardboard and when we cut them out – we had money! Sometimes we did this simply to feel as if we had money of our own.

Other times, for entertainment, if June or I would find a candle, a stub, not a candle of usable length, we would drip the wax. Hot wax was amazing stuff. The solid wax would become a liquid, then as it cooled, it would become a solid again. Rather fascinating for us, actually. We would sometimes drip the hot wax into our hands to see what shape it would make among the creases. The hot wax would sting a bit, but that was part of the excitement. As I've said, it didn't take a lot to entertain us when nothing else was available.

With no electric lines to the house, we could not use our electric powered clothes washer. A relative who lived in town, with electricity, but no washing machine, got it. Mom would take our clothes to the laundry in Topeka to wash them. Of course, June and I could not be left at home and had to go with her. When we got bored and wanted to leave the building, if we asked, she always refused. If we simply left, there was no problem. She never even commented when we returned. She truly was a negligent mother. Her behavior was so typically inconsistent!

We would simply cross the street to the drugstore. In those days it was safer for kids to wander the streets than now. If we had money, even just ten cents, we could buy a comic book. Sometimes we were gone as long as an hour. When we returned, mom made no comment. She never mentioned the comic books. She was not observant – she was not a hands-on mother.

When I was in high school, Mom decided I could do the family laundry. To do that, I was sent to town. Daddy drove me. I don't know what he did while I did the laundry, but I did the laundry alone. I'd been there with Mom, so I knew what to do. I'd had to help her before she sent me alone.

The laundry was in a large room, full of washing machine, each with its own set of rinse tubs. There were pipes just below the ceiling with hoses coming down between the machines. The hoses could be swung from place to place to fill the various machines and tubs. When you needed water, you might have to wait for someone else to finish filling their tubs. There were drains in the floor for the water to run out. It was a hot, wet, and steamy place.

The washing machines had electric motors which ran the agitator in the washtubs and the wringers of the washing machines. After filling the washtub with hot water, and putting in detergent and the dirty clothes, you let it run while you filled the rinse tubs with cold water. When you thought the clothes were clean, you ran them through the wringer to the first rinse tub. Using the wringer was tricky. You had to carefully feed the clothes into it so the fabric would not bunch up and the buttons would not pop off. A missing button would result in screaming by my mother for my carelessness. Then you stirred the clothes in the rinse tub with a stick.

As soon as a load of clothes was out of the washtub, you filled it with clothes again, using the same water. You gradually moved the clothes through the three rinse tubs, each time stirring them with the stick to get the soap out. When the washing was in full swing, the washing machine and all three rinse tubs would be full of clothes in various stages of getting clean.

White clothes were washed first. The first rinse tub they went into had to have some blueing added to the water to bleach the clothes. Colored clothes were washed next, jeans and real dirty socks came last. All the clothes were washed and rinsed in the same water which became dirtier and dirtier as more clothes were washed. When each bunch of clothes was moved to another tub of water, you had to run them through the wringer. That was the most tedious part of the job, and the most dangerous. It was not uncommon for children to playfully stick their fingers in the wringer. Sometimes it would pull their arm off. Children were not supposed to run the machines alone, but some mothers didn't care.

When the clothes had gone through the washer, and the three rinse tubs, they were put through the wringer a final time onto the lid on top of the washing machine, and from there dumped into a waiting clothes basket. I did it exactly the way I'd seen Mom do it, and later we had done it together. The wet clothes were taken home to be hung on a line to dry outside. Daddy had to carry the baskets of wet clothes; they were too heavy for me.

When we got home with the clean clothes, mom never thanked me, but would scream that the clothes were not clean enough. From the intensity of her screaming I always thought she would wash them again to get them clean, but to my surprise, she never did. I never understood.

That is often how I spent my Saturdays while I was in high school.

Then there was the famous water fight. That day only June and I, and older brother Jim, were home. I was a freshman in high school and trying to wash my gym suit. It had to be washed more often than our family did laundry, so I used a pan of water on the kitchen work table. While I was trying to do this, Jim came in and decided to show me how to wash clothes – as if I'd never done that before! His superior attitude was insufferable and soon we were throwing handfuls of water at each other getting the whole kitchen wet.

He finally retreated to his bedroom, but I wasn't finished, so I took the pan of water and poured it under the door into his bedroom. This naturally enraged him further and before he could come out of the room, June and I ran out of the house. We decided to run away to our big sister, Juanita's, only about six miles away. While we were on the road, we recognized the motor of

Jim's car approaching and, since we didn't want him to find us, we hid in the bushes at the side of the road while he roared past. We then, resumed walking.

Before we reached our destination Mom and Daddy came home to find the house in complete chaos and the three of us missing. Mom quickly assessed the situation.

"Jim's killed the girls and stuffed their bodies in the trunk and took off!" She screamed, which Daddy delighted to relate later. At least, when we heard this, we knew she cared.

Daddy managed to persuade Mom that maybe that was NOT actually what had happened, maybe we had just run away. He called some neighbors to help search for us. Juanita's house was our most likely destination, but there were several routes that would take us there, so those roads had to be searched. We were found less than half a mile from our goal. The neighbor took us back home.

Strangely, we were not chastised for the mess we left or running away, Jim's aggravating behavior was well known to everyone in the family.

Jim's behavior was such a problem that shortly after this, Mom insisted that he move out. I don't know the details, but we were all relieved when he was gone. Years later I learned that Daddy paid the expenses of the apartment to make sure he didn't live at home. He was out of high school by this time so he was old enough he should have been able to take care of himself. I didn't know what he did then, I didn't care.

After our older sister, Juanita, began having children, when I was twelve and June was eight, she began to want help. When her first child, Duane, was born it was just babysitting and it was fun. I'd always liked babies and taking care of the baby was fun. A second child, a girl, was born when he was two. Elona Sue was not much more work than Duane, but two years later a third child, Mark, was born. Three children are much more work than one or two and Juanita could not manage.

Juanita began to spend large amounts of time on the couch, just like our mother had done when I was little. I didn't know this was now a family pattern. She would call our mother and tell her to bring me or June, or both of us, to do her work. She even insisted on help to get dressed. When we weren't present, the task of fastening her bra fell on little Duane. He was only two and a half. She continued to insist he do that until he left home at seventeen!

The number of her children increased, there were eventually four; Mark then Bill. A fifth pregnancy did not proceed to term. Everyone was relieved at that. As the number of her children increased, so did the amount and intensity of her screaming. She was so loud, that some summer days, when she was screaming outside the house, her mother-in-law, who lived on the next farm nearly half a mile north, could hear her. There was nothing Lena could do except love the babies more when they came to see her. The children were so desperate for her affection they began to make their way to her house, alone at a young age. Duane was just two and a half when he first trekked through the adjoining pasture to her house. His grandma was surprised! But the trips soon became normal.

The work demanded of us at Juanita's soon advanced from babysitting to cleaning house, cooking and the other chores we did at home. In the summer time, we simply lived there, sleeping on the couch. While we were small, sleeping there, with our heads at each end of the couch, only our feet would get tangled with each other. As we grew bigger that arrangement became less and less possible. There was no extra bed.

I only got out of this work when I left Kansas for college. As I had gotten older I became less and less "manageable," from my older sister's point of view. I began to object to the work and to the specific, and often bizarre, ways she wanted certain tasks accomplished. The procedures she demanded often required more time and effort than was otherwise necessary. It was such a waste of time! I didn't want to be her slave under her control. She NEVER said thank you, nor did she indicate any appreciation for anything that was done for her. Time at her house was thankless and miserable.

I had more than one reason to get away from home. Then I would finally be free!

But nothing was easy or simple, not even dating. When June and I began to date, our mother found another way to embarrass and humiliate us. She was a genius at that! The boy would come for one of us. When we came downstairs to leave, she would stop us and inspect us.

"Your neck is just as dirty as it could be," she would exclaim loudly in front of him. "Now go back upstairs and wash your neck." In warm weather, it was our elbows. Of course, we rushed up and did as we were told. Neither of us had the courage to simply ignore her.

I've never intentionally washed my neck or elbows since!

Singing Career

When June and I were young girls we would sing together. We sang at 4-H Club meetings and we sang at home. Singing was an activity we enjoyed and it helped pass the time while we were working. Oftentimes, at church, when there was time between one activity and another, such as the church service and Sunday School, when people were moving about and visiting, June and I would begin singing impromptu, often in the church basement. We enjoyed the singing and people complimented us for it. It was a rare time when I received any compliments.

"Oh, Sadie," big brother, Jim, said to me one day. "June can sing better than you." He was older, knew more, and was serious. I was trusting and believed him I wish I hadn't. I stopped singing and lost that joy in my life.

Years later, when my children were growing up, I wanted to sing in the church choir. To do that, I wanted to learn to sing, so I took lessons. Unfortunately, the teacher I found could not play the piano so that attempt didn't go far. Still determined to learn, I took formal singing classes at Washburn University. I learned that my brother Jim was wrong. I could sing and quite well. Who made him a judge of singing? No one, but that was typical of the negative tone of my childhood.

My sister, June, did not have the discouragement I faced and, in fact, was encouraged to sing. She sang in local talent shows and special events. She went on to be a music teacher and was often asked to sing at weddings and other similar events. I wonder, if I had been encouraged, could I have become as good a singer as my sister? I don't know why not.

I enjoyed singing so much I eventually sang in the church choir and I would go to nursing homes and sing for the residents. Eventually, age forced me to quit due to the limitations of my throat. My throat could not take the effort. I still regret having to quit.

Careers Teaching School

Teaching school was virtually the only career option open to young women in the nineteenth and early twentieth century. The grandmother I am named after, Sarah Sadie McAllister, taught school. She attended the Normal School program of Campbell University in Holton, KS, her hometown. She taught in several area schools, all one-room country schools, before marrying my grandfather, William Harrison Yoho. How they met and why they lived in Oklahoma is unknown to us now. He had participated in one of the Oklahoma land runs, then returned to settle there. When my mother was born they were living in a dugout there. She remembered the dirt floor and, as a very young girl, seeing a few Native Americans pass by their home wearing their indigenous clothing. When she married social standards expected her to cease teaching, and she did.

My mother began teaching as soon as she could in order to be on her own. If she hadn't, she would have been expected to help her father on the farm. He was a progressive thinker and encouraged her. She taught in rural Oklahoma schools until she married, which was the custom of the times. After she married she did not teach again until her youngest was old enough to attend school herself and social norms had changed. When mom first began teaching only single, unmarried women could teach. World War II changed that with so many men away, women had to fill their roles. In 1953 she easily resumed teaching because she had a lifetime certificate from Oklahoma which Kansas honored. A few years later, though, these were not honored and those teachers had to return to college. To do this, she rode with my brother, Don, when he began to attend Washburn University in Topeka. She obtained her bachelors degree in education in 1957.

"You can always teach," Mom would say as she encouraged all of us children to also teach. She considered it the easiest and most available job in the world. Neither are true. I did get a degree though, yet I wondered, if I was not so smart, how could I have done that? And, how could I teach? But, I had the piece of paper and did teach. All my brothers and our younger sister also taught. June and I taught the longest of all of us.

My brothers taught the least before going on to other occupations. We have a long line of educators in the family, now a great granddaughter of hers is teaching.

Mom had encouraged her grandchildren to teach, but only two went into education. Of them, only one taught. Her influence on us all was remarkable. Only later, did we learn she truly was a poor teacher. One former student related that she learned very little her fifth grade year when mom was her teacher. Many afternoons, mom would give the class an assignment to keep them busy. Then she would stand a large book up, open, on her desk as if to read it. Instead of reading, she would lay her head down on her arms on the desk – and go to sleep!

When the students would notice she was quiet, and not moving, the bravest one would silently tip toe to her desk. When he would see that she was asleep, he would signal to the rest of the class. They became absolutely quiet at this point in order to let her sleep as long as possible. This was not out of respect or compassion. As long as she was asleep – she could not assign them more work to do! They learned very little.

The principal of the school would walk down the hall, notice the silence in her classroom, evidence that the students were not loud or disorderly, and walk on – satisfied that mom was an EXCELLENT teacher!! How odd. And, she did this for years! That can't be done nowadays.

Later, I taught at that same school, with some of the same staff. A janitor from her time and I were talking once, and he said even he knew mom slept in front of the class. I was amazed!

Once my children had left home, on their own, and I no longer needed to support them, I stopped teaching in order to explore other aspects of life. During one of those later jobs, I learned I was dyslexic. If I had known about dyslexia while I was teaching, I could have helped so many students so much more. I was a remedial reading teaching, yet information on dyslexia was so sparse, I knew nothing about it. Many teachers, and other people, still don't.

Attending School

We walked to school. Our school, Williams, was two and a half miles away if going on the roads. If we walked through the fields it was only a mile and a half. Sometimes we would walk that way, but there were creeks to cross, with all their mud and water, fields to walk through, and barbed wire fences to get through (they were tricky, especially while wearing a skirt or dress!). Walking on the road, though longer, was easier, especially in bad weather or snow when the roads would at least have tracks to walk in. When we got to school before classes started, we would play outside, just like recess!

When I first started school, Don and Jim also still attended. They were big boys and had bikes which they rode. I had to walk. Sometimes Don would walk with me and I wanted him to hold my hand, but he wouldn't. I'm sure he thought that wasn't what a big boy did.

Ours was a one room school, so all classes were in the same room and there was just one teacher. There were not many children in each class, maybe just two or three, sometimes even just one. The school day began by pledging allegiance to the flag of the United States of America. You faced the flag, you put your hand over your heart and we all recited the pledge together. I don't remember the controversy when the phrase, "under God," was added. It was, and still is, reasonable to me. In addition, some teachers would read a short prayer.

Lunch was not served by the school, we each had to take our own. Mom did not give much attention to our lunches. If we had anything at all to take, we felt lucky. We took whatever was on hand. One day we might take half a dozen molasses cookies (the only kind we were allowed to make, Mom thought they were healthier), another day it may be several apples, or even doughnuts we had made. But what we took was not our entire lunch. We were more resourceful than that. We traded. We traded for other student's food. An apple would get half a sandwich. We ended with a more balanced meal.

One unforgettable day mom opened a can of meat for sandwiches only to discover we were out of bread. She had taken the meat out of the can, so she put it back into the can and drove to the store to get bread. She sat the can in the cupboard, not the icebox, while she went to get the bread. When she returned we made sandwiches and went on to school.

That day Don and Jim ate two sandwiches while I ate only half of one. When school was out Jim began to ride his bike home when he fell to the ground writhing in pain. The teacher came out intending to go home, instead he put Jim and his bike in the back of his truck to take Jim home. Since Don and I lived there too, he took us with them. By the time we got home, Don was also sick and I soon followed.

The boys were sicker than I was. The conclusion was that the meat had gone bad in the time it sat warm in the opened can. I had eaten less, so I did not get as sick. No one else had eaten any of the mean, no one else was sick that day. After that, Mom was more careful with food in opened cans. Most of the time we took peanut butter sandwiches with the peanut butter mixed with syrup.

Sometimes, Jim would be instructed, on the way to school, to ride his bike to the neighborhood store, three miles away, to purchase something for our lunches. Don had gone on to high school by then. Jim would get food for us, myself and June, but he would get something special just for himself – and he made sure we knew it. This was typical of Jim.

As we walked to school, we went past a shack that an old man lived in all by himself. He was related to the man who owned the neighborhood grocery store, both knew who we were. In his front yard was a big pear tree. On the way past we would go into his yard and pick up pears for lunch. He told us if we picked the ones on the ground we could have all we wanted. This is where we got the pears. They were a great addition to our lunches.

One day an older girl brought a new and unique writing instrument to school. I'd heard of such things, but never seen one before. It was a wonderful kind of pen, a ballpoint pen; the first we'd ever seen. Everyone wanted to write with it. It was passed around so everyone could write a little something. The ink came out so smooth and easily, and made much straighter lines than the pens we were used to. It had its own ink!

When the pen came to me I tried to write with it, but so many others had used it ahead of me that it ran out of ink. I was puzzled and disappointed. The girl who brought the pen was outraged and screamed at me that I had ruined her special pen and I had to buy her a new one. I had no idea where to find one, nor did I have any money to buy one if I had known where to find them. I knew the pens were expensive, several dollars each, and I had no money at all. It took a long time for her to stop blaming me for "ruining" her pen.

One time, in the fifth grade, for some reason I can't recall, a test I had to take was read to me. The one giving the test was a teacher, but not my teacher. She lived in the neighborhood, so I knew who she was at the time, but can't remember her name now. As she read the questions, I quickly stated the answers – and they were correct. It was the most enjoyable test I'd ever taken.

"If she hears the questions," I heard her say after the test. "She can answer them. She is smart." I was shocked to hear that. For the first time in my life someone had said that I was smart. How could that be?

Would I get help now for the things that were difficult? No one ever read a test to me again, and I never got help. Both are common now for dyslexic students.

Most years were otherwise uneventful, but my eighth grade year was not. My mother had returned to teaching that year. And, unfortunately, that year she was my teacher. She had been out of practice teaching for twenty years. And that year, she did not teach at a school near our home, but one nearly thirty miles away. For some reason, that likely made sense only to her, she decided to take June and myself with her. It was not a good year. That year, June and I spent every minute of every day with her. That was worse than no fun!

On the way to school, about an hour drive, Mom would complain – constantly. On the way home she complained about how the day went. I'm sure her expectations for that year were based on the best memories of teaching when she was younger and had more energy. For June and me it was wearing. Her complaining was normal and depressing.

That year she didn't teach me much. I don't know that she even tried. She was convinced I was "slow," so why should she waste time on me? Needless to say, I didn't learn much. She did, though, pass me on to high School. I guess I wasn't too "slow" for that! None of it made any sense to me.

In those years every grade school held a school play for Christmas. And, every year, the eighth graders would get the major parts. I was looking forward to this school treat. My mother was my teacher that year and, for reasons she never explained, not only did I NOT get a major part in the play – I had no part at all! I was assigned to read a poem, separate from the play. I still don't know why she did that.

My first day of high school was a half day. When I arrived home, earlier than expected, I decided to go to Williams school, where June attended, to surprise her and we could walk home together. June was delighted with my surprise visit. We had a great time walking home and sharing about our unusual first days: her first day of going to school alone, my first day of the big school in town. When mom got home she screamed at me, insisting that I should have stayed home and worked. That's all that was important to her.

At Highland Park High School, the big city high school that I attended, I felt like a country hick. Going from a one room country school to a high school in town, was difficult at the very least. It was hard to fit in; I never felt I did. The contrast between the small rural school with only about twenty students in all eight grades and then the town school of five hundred, was enormous.

It seemed to me that all the other girls were city girls and knew each other. I'm sure now that that was not true, but I had no way to know otherwise at the time. Consequently, I did not make much effort to make friends. No one knowing me now would ever guess that. Years after I'd left high school I learned that other people were interesting and wanted to be friends as much as I did.

Starting at Highland Park, feeling I was the only outsider, and having been told I was "slow" and not able to achieve much, I kept to myself. I could never act like the other kids because my life was so different from theirs. I could never feel as carefree as they acted. Of course they were "immature" in my eyes; they didn't have the responsibilities at home that I did. They acted like children, because they were. It seemed to me that they lived lives of luxury because I was sure they didn't have to do the work at home that I did. Despite their childish behavior, I felt out-classed by them, their confidence and their nice clothes. I figured none of the wealthy, smart city girls would want to be friends with someone as dumb and slow as I was told, and believed, myself to be. This was true of college too.

I didn't know how wrong I was.

The other girls obviously had more money than I did, at least more was spent on their clothes, and they had accessories; I did not. I made all my own clothes, but didn't consider that to be any kind of achievement. It was necessity. I'd made my own clothes for years. That was normal.

I wanted to learn – odd for a "slow" student, isn't it? But since I was slow, I didn't take classes I was really interested in. Instead, I took a class I thought I could pass, such as Home Ec. There, in the sewing unit, I hemmed a tiny tea towel. For the other girls, this was a challenge. I had just finished making a two-piece, double breasted suit, on my own! I was so bored with that tea towel!! What a waste of my time! I could have actually learned something, and enjoyed it, in a different class!

Despite all that, I enjoyed being at the high school. I didn't want to go home. Nearly every day I figured out a reason to stay at school beyond class time. Often I would play basketball with other girls. That, I enjoyed. And, I learned, for the very first time, to be assertive. I had to be in order to get control of the ball. I learned to fight for the ball! For the first time in my life, asserting myself was not a crime. It was amazing!

I didn't have the courage to join any specific after-school activity, and I was sure my mother would explode if I did, but I managed to stay at school, just the same. Buses left at two times to take students home; one right after classes were out, the other left after the after-school activities. I nearly always took the later one home. Once I was home, I was expected to work – and I was so tired of that! This extra time at school gave me my first free time. It was great!

During my Junior year, the time came to order the class rings. I really wanted one so I could be like the other kids. Daddy understood my need and gave me the huge sum of $15.00 for the ring. In 1957 that was a significant amount of money. I was so excited!! I could be like the (to me) rich city kids!

Before I could take the money to school, however, Mom decided she needed it to pay for that year's baby chicks. She said, in return, that I could have some of the money when we sold the eggs. She made it sound so reasonable and I trusted her. I was never allowed to object, anyway. It never happened. I never got any money from the eggs, and I didn't get the ring. Typical.

The next year, I tried again. Daddy understood how critical it was now, and again, gave me the money. Wouldn't you know it – again, Mom decided she needed the money for something. This time, I rebelled. It was too much! I refused. She became angry, but got over it. I did get the ring, but now I had only part of my Senior year to wear it. It would have been more exciting to have gotten it with the rest of the kids! Then, I could have felt I <u>belonged</u>!

I wonder now, if she might have been jealous. She never had a class ring that I know of. But, I couldn't think about it at the time. There was a lot she didn't have in her life, how could she let me have those things? I couldn't see her side then though.

High school could have been exciting, but I didn't know how, or have the confidence, for that to happen. I eventually learned, but later in my life.

June and I managed one little extravagance about this time. We bought the first portable, transistor radio in the family. The family had a radio, it was in the living room, on a small table. The chairs around it were the best place to listen, but you had to pay close attention. My older brother liked to listen to westerns mostly: The Lone Ranger, Gunsmoke, Bobby of the B-Bar-B (ranch), Sergeant Preston of the Yukon, even Big John and Little Sparky. I only caught bits and pieces of the shows while I was working. I wasn't allowed to sit beside the radio and listen. The programs were on at various times and days during the week. Occasionally, I could hear the gun shots and sounds of violence from the westerns and didn't think they were good for Jim to be involved with, he was violent enough anyway, but I had no right to comment. One time, though, I was able to listen to most of one program and found myself drawn into the story. From then on, I wanted to listen more often, but I had work to do – he didn't.

We had this radio before the electric lines reached our house. It was a battery-powered radio. The battery for it, there was only one, was larger than a car battery! We didn't think of it as unusually large at the time, it was just the size that batteries were! Thinking of it now, it was huge! Anyway, as all batteries do, it eventually died. That was the end of listening to the radio.

Sometime after the battery had been dead for a while, several of us were in the room looking at the radio and talking about not being able to listen to any programs at all. Daddy walked into the room, to the radio, and stood beside it.

"Why don't you just turn it on?" He asked casually as he turned the power knob. The radio boomed to life, stunning us all! He chuckled in delight at our surprise. He had secretly replaced the battery when no one was around and had waited for such a moment as this to turn it on! We were astonished and delighted! Still, it was not my choice what was listened to.

By the time I was in high school, I hatched a plan and invited June to join me in it. I needed her help, but she could share in the reward. She was excited about the possibility. We saved the meager amount of money that came our way, then: we bought our **own** radio! One of the new transistor radios! They were amazingly tiny and so easy to carry! It could be taken anywhere.

On a trip to town she and I went to a local appliance store and picked it out ourselves. We had saved the money (I don't remember now how we managed to do that!), our parents had no role, or veto of this independent act! The radio we picked was salmon colored. It being pink was enough to discourage our older brother from wanting it! We listened to rock and roll music, but not too loud. It was our private pride and joy.

I've wondered whatever happened to it. I didn't take it with me when I left home, June was still there to listen to it. Did she take it when she left home? I suppose, but I've not thought to ask her about it. Maybe it simply became part of the family junk stored in a box somewhere. I don't know, but I'm sure it's gone now. I do know how victorious we felt to have this radio, our own first thing! It was our independence and we reveled in it!

Chick Mate

In the summer we always had baby chickens, most often they were bought from a hatchery. One summer a hen of ours hatched out some chicks. She had made a nest where none of us could find it. Ours were truly free range chickens! This didn't happen very often because Mom wouldn't let the hens sit on the eggs long enough to hatch. She preferred to sell the eggs and buy the chicks. I never understood why and, of course, she never explained.

I was watching this hen and her chicks when I noticed one chick walked with a limp. I picked it up and took it to the house. I put the chick in a box on the porch and kept it over night. The next day it walked just fine, so I thought it was healed and took it back to the mother hen. There, it started limping again. So, I took it back to the house and kept it in the box. Every night I had to put it to bed. I would hold it gently, rock it and wrap it in its towel. After that it mostly lived on the porch.

One evening, June and I were playing on the swings and Mom was sitting in the front yard. Baby chick wanted someone to put her to bed. She walked around and around Mom cheeping to get her attention. Mom would have nothing to do with it, so called me to come put chick to bed. I did, the chick was content and went to sleep. It had become attached to human attention.

The evening while I was sick from poisoned food, I was unable to put Baby Chick to bed as usual. We were sleeping outside on a mattress on the ground because it was so hot in the house. This was before air conditioning was affordable and we had no fan. Other families had at least a fan, but not us. I don't know why.

Baby Chick came from the porch to get in bed with me. When I was falling asleep my hands relaxed from cuddling the chick. I was barely aware that it happened and too sick to stop it. It crawled under the sheet and roosted on my leg. Mom noticed the lump on my leg and knew it was the chick. While there, it pooped on my leg. When mom discovered this, she cleaned my leg than returned the chick to the chicken house. She wasn't going to take care of it. She could tolerate something that required her attention.

Later, after I was well, I went to the chicken house, hoping to find my chick, I could not. It looked like all the other chicks. I thought it would recognize me, but it did not. I was disappointed, but there was nothing I could do. That was the end of my chick mate, but not the end of my experience with domestic birds.

When I was grade school age the city of Topeka would have pet parades where children could walk down the center of the street with their pets. This intrigued me from the time I first learned of these parades. How exciting I thought it would be to do that! When I was about eleven, I figured out a plan and persuaded Daddy to take June and me to be part of the pet parade. Choosing a pet was not the easiest part. We didn't really have any pets.

We had animals all over our farm, surely I would be able to take one in the parade. We had chickens and turkeys roaming all around the house and barn, cows for milk and dogs to ward off coyotes and other predators. We each had to pick one of them to be our "pet" to be in the parade. June chose the dog. Our dogs were always large dogs, to be a match for the coyotes. This year the dog was not fully grown, but was a recognizable "pet." We had cats, but they were somewhat wild. They had to be to hunt mice to stay alive.

What would I take?

It had to be different from the dog.

A chicken?

My chick-mate was lost, so that was not an option.

A milk cow?

That was no pet! Besides, it was too large to get easily in or out of the pickup truck, which was the only vehicle available to transport animals.

A cat?

A cat was too independent. We had no cage, so the animal would have to be able to mind itself, and certainly none of our cats certainly would do that.

The only reasonable possibility was – a turkey. There were no other options.

That day, for the parade, a turkey would be my pet!

The turkey was a challenge, though. But all the work I had to do normally was a challenge, that was nothing unusual. First was the size of the bird. Turkeys were so large, and I was so small, that I couldn't pick up or carry one. And, they do have a mind of their own, no matter how pea-brained it might be, but I had no other choice! Other children were able to do this, and I was so tired of being left out of all the fun. I was going to do it!

On the day of the parade the dog was happy to get into the back of the pickup, and smart enough to stay there when we told it to. He enjoyed the trip. The turkey, we managed to get into the cab of the truck and it squatted down on the floor in fear once the truck started. It tried to move as we drove, but I was able to hold it in place. What did my parents think of my taking a turkey? I have no idea, or at least no memory of it now.

We got to town and to the parade site without incident, though there was turkey poop on the floor of the truck, but – so what about that? We were used to that all over the yard and knew how to be careful not to step in it.

Amazingly, without any kind of leash or control, the turkey followed and walked beside me down the street in the parade. It was WONDERFUL!! For once in my life, I got to do what I'd seen other kids do! It was like a dream! I was like a normal kid! That, in itself was exciting.

I can only think, now, that the turkey stayed by me and didn't run away because the crowds of people on both sides of the street were more terrifying than anything it had ever experienced. I doubt it thought of me as its owner, though I was more familiar to it than any of the crowd of people. I certainly wasn't its "master," nor was it trained in any way to stay with me. Actually, that it did stay with me was a kind of miracle.

In fact, turkeys do not take to being herded very well – usually, not at all.

After the parade was over, we managed to get the turkey back into the cab of the truck. Then June and I persuaded Daddy to take us up to the top of the dome of the State House. We saw other people up there. They waved to us and we waved back. They were so tiny, it was amazing! We were in town and had no pressing errands to do, and mom wasn't with us to say, "no." In those days there was unlimited access to the dome. We couldn't leave the dog in the back of the truck, so he went with us! No one stopped us. Was ours the only dog to go up to the top of the dome? I don't know.

The view of the city from the top was astonishing. The buildings looked like toys. The cars and trucks were very tiny toys, and the people… People looked like bugs!! Smaller than ants, which we stepped on easily! And the wind was different from what we felt on the ground, but it was the view that stayed in my mind. I never forgot that breathtaking experience. Thank you, Daddy!

We went home to our normal drab life, but I had been in a parade – with **my** "pet" turkey!

School Games

We always played games at school outside of class time. Our playground was large so we had lots of room to play anything we wanted. One game we played was 'Dixie.' I don't know why it was called that, it just was. We would have a board or rock in the middle of the playground to indicate it was the "jail." At opposite ends of the playground we made a line in the dirt to mark the safe zone. Two or three kids would guard the jail and try to catch the runners while the other kids would run back and forth from one safe place to another. If you got caught, you had to go to jail. Other kids would then try to get you free and pull you out of jail. Sometimes all the kids got caught and game would start over. There was a lot of running!

Another game we played was called 'Blackman.' I don't know the reason for that name either, it's just what we called it. The name didn't mean anything to us. In it, three or four kids would run around trying to "tag" others. If you got tagged you would have join those who were tagging others.

If we weren't playing these games, in warm weather we would play softball. I thought playing softball was better than eating. We would divide up sides to play. Two of the boys would be captains of the two teams and then chose kids to be on their team. The better players were always chosen first. I always was chosen in the middle, but I played as hard as I could. I was glad never to be chosen last, or even near the end. I didn't realize, then, that that indicated a level of acceptance which I didn't often feel. I could play ball.

I didn't have a glove so I would borrow one. I would throw the ball with my left hand. Most of the kids were right handed so I had to borrow a right handed glove and when I caught the ball I would take the glove off and throw. It slowed me down a little. When I went to bat, though, I batted right handed. I had two hands and used both of them.

Every so often, on a Friday afternoon, we would go to another school and play softball with their team. One time we went to this school to play softball and our teacher's name caused a showdown. His last name was, "Snell." A few of the older boys would refer to him as, "Snellbacher," a German name they considered derogatory – since we had been fighting Germany in

World War Two, as if his family had shortened their name to hide that heritage. This time an older student at my school, called him Mr. "Snellbacher" in front of the other teachers. When we got back to our school Mr. Snell tried to make John use his correct name.

"My name is Snell," he said.

"Bacher," John shot back. John was as big as the teacher, what could he do? I don't remember how the incident ended, but I don't think he was expelled from school. I think he should have been.

One year, on the last day of school, we wanted to play softball. We usually wore jeans on the last day of school, but this year Kitty Ramsey and I had worn dresses. We had brought jeans and needed to change. The teacher lived in a small trailer beside the school, so Kitty and I went into her trailer to change clothes. Kitty took off her dress. I could see she wore a nice slip and other undergarments. I had only a pair of panties. I quickly decided I was not going to take my dress off. I didn't want her to see that I wasn't wearing a slip. I quickly said I didn't want to play, and went home. I never told her the reason. It never occurred to me that I could explain that I had no choice in the clothes I wore. My mother, who wasn't interested in her own clothes, certainly didn't care much about what I had to wear. I was trapped in her limitations.

Reading

In the spring of my first year of school I was learning to read. I was so excited! I'd been told I couldn't learn, but here I was – learning! On the top of one worksheet page the teacher put a star because I read all the words without making a mistake. I was bursting with excitement to show Mom. I just knew she would be so happy for me! This was my most astonishing accomplishment – and I'd been told I couldn't do it! The almost two mile walk home that day seemed to take FOREVER!

When I finally got home, I found Mom in the garden pulling weeds, not a happy task. I proudly showed her my page with the star on it.

"What does that mean?" She asked.

'She was a teacher,' I thought. 'Why doesn't she know what it means?'

"It means I read that page without missing a word!" I was eager to hear her praise this amazing accomplishment. Instead, she shrugged her shoulders and turned back to her weeds. I was absolutely devastated!! She couldn't have hurt me more if she stabbed me in the back and turned the blade. I had achieved this amazing accomplishment – and she didn't care! I was stunned. That's all the support I got. I didn't bother showing her any papers after that. What was the point?

The year I was in the 4th grade there was also one boy, Kenny, in my grade. That was all. There were just the two of us. He was smart and the teacher would explain the lesson to him and he would, in turn, explain it to me. Once I understood the lesson, I had it. At the end of the year the teacher decided that if I took the 4th grade over again, and Kenny moved on to the 6th grade with some other boys, there would be no reason to teach fifth grade lessons. This decision put me back in the 4th grade again, but this time with Kenny's little sister Kitty.

"Sadie is slow," my mother said when she heard of this proposal. "It would be good for her," she agreed. I, the trusting child, believed it. I had no voice to object, anyway. But, it wasn't "good" for me – it was just the opposite.

Kitty liked to play, so that's what we did. I already knew all the material, so I didn't need to study. I just had to learn the spelling words over again. I could never remember the spelling words. I would study the words all week, take the test and forget them. I would start studying the next week's words, take that test and forget those words. I did this week after week, year after year. I think I wasted my time. I got A's in spelling, but I didn't learn the reasons words were spelled they way they were, and there was no context for using the words, so there was no meaning behind the rote memorization – and no retention. I still can't spell.

Not having to study that second year in the 4th grade made it easy to not study from then on. If Kitty didn't want to study, we would play. This set a pattern for me not to study. However, one night Mom decided she would help me with an English lesson. On this one page there was a box that had some sentences in it. I was to read the sentences without making a mistake. There were two words that I could not remember. I could only read by memory. I read the sentences and would miss a word. So, I had to read it again. I would read it again and miss another word. So, I read it again and missed another word. Her watching me did not help. I made more mistakes knowing she would be critical. That just intensified the downward spiral.

Her patience snapped and she began to scream at me to read all the words right. The screaming did not help. I would miss one word one time and another word another time. I was now even missing words I knew. The situation deteriorated to chaos and frustration on both sides. Finally, she got tired of screaming at me and let me go to bed. So much for helping me with my English lesson!

I didn't know how to sound out words. I didn't have any idea what the different letters sounded like. Mom knew I didn't know phonics but did nothing to help me. She would laugh or make fun of me when I would mispronounce a word. To this day I don't understand why, since she was a teacher, she wouldn't help me. I guess, once she had decided it was a good thing I was pretty because I wasn't very smart, it wouldn't have done any good to help me. I did learn to read one word at a time. But to this day I cannot spell.

I had no idea what to do with a vowel. The inconsistent English pronunciation of them does not help. I didn't know then that many words in the English language have been taken from other languages, retaining some of the original pronunciation, so there is no consistency in pronunciation. I eventually learned to read books and enjoy them. I still do.

In the summer Mom would take June and me to the library to get books. That was the nicest thing she did for us. I don't know what I would have done without those books. In a book, I could escape – and I certainly needed to escape. June and I both read a lot, but June was the smart one; she just wasn't very pretty, or so Mom said. Would Mom have taken me if June wasn't there? I doubt it.

I still remember some of the books we read. I say "we" because June and I would read not only the books we had each checked out, but the other's books as well. Many of the books we read were books in a series. One series was the Silhouette books. In the front of each volume was a silhouette of the person the book was about. They were biographies of famous people. I enjoyed learning about real people's lives. They faced challenges too! The frontispiece of each book had a silhouette of the subject of the book. Then, each chapter page had an additional silhouette of something which continued the theme of the series. Most of the people who were the subjects of these books were famous and I knew about them before-hand, others I learned about simply by reading these books. I read to learn, I still do.

We also read the books by Lois Linsky and all seven of the Oz books. They are far more involved than just Dorothy's accidental trip to Oz. The many characters, and their various adventures, were fascinating. I was especially taken by a princess who had many different heads, one to fit each mood she may have been feeling at the time. That idea amazed me then, and still does. I still don't know how the author could have imagined such things.

When I read a book I become so engrossed in the story that I imagine I am part of the story. I truly entered the world of the book. This should be no surprise. My daily home life was so unpleasant, I was desperate to get away. A book was a safe place to go, however briefly. It didn't matter if I could be in the world of the story for only a few moments, every brief moment away was precious. But, I could keep the world of the story in my head as I did my work, so the experience of the story carried beyond its reading.

Before we had a TV, or any other forms of diversion (if we had a radio it was off limits to me, and we never had a phonograph player), reading was the only alternative to work that I was allowed. I'm not sure why my mother even allowed that. And, if I was so "slow," as she so often said, why would I even want to read? I never thought of those inconsistencies then, but now they have become apparent. Mentally slow learners don't often like to read, it is too difficult to follow the story. I read eagerly. Even if the reading might have been risky, I read. When June and I finished our library books, and it would be days before we could go back to the library and get more, we became desperate for something to read. There were few other books in the house.

Our brother, Jim, had some books. They were some of the Hardy boys series. We didn't care if they were "boys books," we were desperate to read. But we were sure he would deny us permission if we asked, so we had to work around that. When we were sure he would not know, we would sneak one book out of the room he shared with his brothers, read it as quickly as possible, then return it just as stealthy. We tried to avoid contact with him as much as possible. We eventually read all of his books and he never knew! It is curious, though, that he was able to own his own books – and we weren't. How odd.

Eventually we got a TV while I was in high school, but I still preferred to read. One day a neighbor came with a TV he wanted to sell. He left it a few days so we could see what was on. Mom refused to buy it, but later changed her mind and bought one, but not his. I remember watching the news with her and one other program, a variety show with Sid Caesar and Imogene Coca, but it was never a major part of our family live.

Though I was the "slow" one, the fifth of six children, I was the first of us to graduate from college. Isn't that odd? How could that have been possibly if I was truly "slow"? Something else must have been going one, but no one considered that. I think my graduating stimulated my brothers to return to college and finish. They, myself and my younger sister, all taught school for a time. Only my sister and I made a career of it though. Some-times I wonder why.

According to my mother, teaching was the only job one could consider. It did give me the same schedule as my children when I became solely responsible for them. But after twenty-two years, teaching eventually wore me down. It's been compared to battle fatigue of combat troops. There are lots of similarities.

First Train Trip

On my tenth birthday we got on the train and went to Carlsbad Cavern. It was our first, and only, big family trip and my first train trip. I was so excited!!! Mom, Daddy, Juanita, Don, Jim, June, and I went. Stanley stayed home to take care of the farm. We could all ride the train with a free pass because Daddy worked for the Santa Fe railroad. We got on the train during daylight and rode all night. In the morning we rode a little before arriving at Carlsbad where we got off. From the station we walked to the cave. I don't remember how far we walked, but the distance didn't matter, we walked.

The complex of tunnels and caves known Carlsbad Cavern was "discovered" in 1898 by a teenager, Jim White. Its existence had been known by residents of the area, but it was considered only a local natural feature until then. He descended into the cavern using a home-made wire ladder, explored and named many of the most accessible spaces and their features. New discoveries continue to be made.

The series of caverns was created by sulfuric acid wending its way through limestone that had been formed about two-hundred and fifty million years ago on the edge of an inland sea as part of a reef complex. Geologic forces eventually pushed this rock, and much of the surrounding land, above sea level about seventeen to twenty million years ago creating the Guadalupe Mountains. Over the millennia these mountains were eroded down. In that process, brine from lower oil and gas deposits was forced into the outer layers of the limestone. The hydrogen sulfide combined with rainwater, and its oxygen, and sulfuric acid was created which began to dissolve the stone. Caves and passages were created. As the land continued to rise, the water-acid mixture drained away, and was replaced by fresh, clean rainwater. The minerals which were left behind created "decorations" on the walls, ceilings and floors of the caverns. They created the stalactites (which hold "tight" to the ceiling), stalagmites (which start on the floor and "might" reach the ceiling), columns (where stalagmites have joined stalactites), "draperies," "soda straws," "popcorn," and the many other formations which are not found above ground.

There are many other caves in the area, created the same way, but none are as large, extensive and adapted to pedestrians, as the ones named after the nearby town. The town is named after the European town of "Charles' Bath," or Karlsbad, originally German, now Karlovy Vary, in the Czech Republic.

Once we got into the cavern we had to walk all the way down into the cave, about seventy-nine stories down. It was exhausting, especially for myself and June. It seemed to go forever! Once down at the bottom, we walked around in the cave, then had to walk all the way back up. Two elevators and an underground lunchroom had been added in 1932, as part of the new visitors center, but for some reason we couldn't use the elevators. June was so little and so tired, Daddy had to carry her most of the way up and out. I wished I could have been carried!

That evening, Juanita took June and me back home on the train by ourselves. We were so tired we easily slept in our seats. Shortly after we woke, we were home! Mom, Daddy and the two boys took the train in the other direction and went on to California. I don't know why we girls were sent back home, except that the others were going to stay with relatives and they likely did not have had enough room for all of us. Any trip with two children is simpler, and far cheaper, than a trip with five or six!

Later, I rode the train many times, but that first trip stands out as special. Even though it wasn't all of us, it was the only family vacation we ever had! I still enjoy riding the train.

Thirty years later, again on my birthday, I took my own two children to the cavern. This time I drove and we rode the elevator. Everyone rides it up, no one rides it down. That trip was just as fun as the first one!

My First Dress

When I was ten I made my first dress. This was not as simple as it may sound. We had an electric sewing machine but, since the electric lines did not reach our house during the war, it was traded with a relative in town for a treadle machine. This machine was powered by the feet of the one doing the sewing.

The need to make our own clothes was imperative because ready-made clothes were too expensive and, due to the war, few were available. Because this would be my first dress, feed sack cloth was used. The feed for our chickens came in rough cloth which had printed patterns on it. These patterns were most often flowers, usually small ones. During the Great Depression the only cloth available to most women for making clothes was this feed sack cloth. So mom took me to the feed store to pick out feed in a pattern I liked. The cloth and their patterns were instantly recognizable as feed sacks, but their use was common so this was not unusual. I chose small, red roses.

We took the sacks of feed, with my roses, home and I had to wait until the chickens ate all the feed before I could use the cloth. After the sacks were empty we had to unravel the seam which formed the sack. The sack was made of one large square of fabric folded in half and sewed together on the bottom and one side. The top seam was sown separately from the side seam so the sack could be opened without undoing the entire thing. The string from both seams was saved for other uses.

The fabric had to be washed thoroughly before being used to make clothes because the feed was dusty with minute bits of grain, dirt and plant material. You did not want to sew this into your clothes, it would be too itchy to wear. I'm sure mom laid out the pattern pieces to get the most use out of the fabric available. She knew the size of fabric used in each feed sack and was able to accurately estimate ahead of time how many sacks a piece of clothing would take. I didn't realize it at the time, but that was an astute ability.

My dress would take two feed sacks. A dress for her would require three feed sacks, maybe four. After she laid out the pieces, she cut them out. Later, when I had more experience and my dexterity improved, I would do this myself.

This dress was not the first piece of clothing I made, but it was the first piece I would wear. The first clothing I made were dresses for my dolls. These were very simple, almost shapeless garments that I could fit my dolls into. Because the dolls were pretend, the clothes were too. I made their clothes out of scraps left over from my mother's sewing. Shapeless though they were, these doll clothes gave me practice using the treadle sewing machine.

A treadle sewing machine was powered by the operator's foot. The treadle was a movable metal platform a few inches above the floor. You braced one foot on the floor with the other on the treadle and pushed down gently on the treadle. You let your foot up, that released pressure, then pushed down again. This action moved the sewing needle up and down and advanced the cloth past the needle. The speed of your foot determined the speed of the needle and the speed of the sewing. The more competent and coordinated a person was, the faster the sewing went. If you could not create and maintain a steady rhythm, the sewing would be jerky and your seams would be crooked. That could make the clothes not fit, and would certainly look sloppy. Straight and steady seams were the goal, and I mastered that! And keep your fingers out of the way of the needle!

My big sister, Juanita, also helped. She gradually took over our mother's role, but then, she liked to take over things. Bluntly: she was bossy. By ten years old, I was used to this. I did not realize that her actual expertise in this case, as opposed to her often assumed expertise, would truly be benefial to me. She would insist that my seams be straight. I would have to rip them out and do them over if they were not straight enough. Eventually I became very proficient in making straight seams. It was not too many years that I began to realize I was a better seamstress than my mother, because she did not care so much if her seams were straight or not. It was not often that I, or anyone else, benefited from my big sisters bossiness. This was one exception.

I did so well on this first dress that mom decided my second dress could be made of regular store fabric. This was a major indication of proficiency on my part. We went to the fabric store for fabric for the rest of my sewing. While still in elementary school I won my first award for sewing at the county 4-H fair. By the time I reached eighth grade I was competent and confident enough to make a double-breasted dress. Double breasted suits were the fashion for men and women. The large lapels folded over each other to be buttoned up. It opened at the side with a zipper. The fabric I chose, for warmth, was corduroy. I never realized that few other girls in high school were able to do this. If I had, I might have had more confidence. But, that day, too, eventually came! It's my time now!

Food Preparation

Food was a constant concern. There was never enough of it. We couldn't afford to buy much food, so we had to grow it and preserve it ourselves. This was common in our neighborhood.

We always had a garden and grew the vegetables we ate. Sometimes we would trade with neighbors, but generally, if we didn't grow it – we didn't eat it. Life was that basic. If you wanted to eat food past the growing season, you had to preserve it. We couldn't afford to buy much canned food. And, frozen food was beyond imagination. No one had home freezers, they did not exist. When home freezers became available, they were large and too costly for my family. Now they are so common, and in different sizes, no one thinks anything about them.

Home preservation of food during the war became critical, and more complicated due to rationing. Sugar was severely rationed. In one of my moves recently, I happened to find my grandfather's ration book for sugar. Each rationed commodity had its own separate book. The coupons in it would be redeemed when you bought that item. The books were issued based on your age and the number in your family. I don't think income had anything to do with it. You could only purchase as much of a commodity as you had coupons for. It was a system to limit consumption of certain products so that the rest could go for the war effort. I remember ration books for sugar, meat and butter.

For "the war effort" we also saved tin foil and flattened tin cans. Recycling was patriotic! We even saved gum wrapper foil, but didn't know what to do with it. I was so young, it was all sort of a game. For adults, though, it was no game.

Preserving food was certainly no game. Canning was the preferred method of preservation because that allowed the food to stay good for the longest time, even years. Canning food at home was much, much cheaper than buying it canned from a store. Food was seldom dehydrated and freezing was not even an option.

Canning vegetables, such as green beans, was simple: pick, clean and trim the ends of the beans, pack them into a canning jar, put in a little salt, fill the jar nearly full of water, then boil in a pan of water for a certain length of time, extract the hot jars carefully and set them out in the air to cool slowly and wait for the tops to pop. It was exciting to hear them pop one at a time. It meant you would have food the next winter. That "pop" meant the lids had sealed. If they did not seal, we set those aside to eat quickly, or re-do the process, but the second time around the vegetables would begin to become mushy, so we tried to avoid that.

When the jars had cooled, we took them down to the basement and filled the shelves down there. As the summer progressed, and the shelves became more and more full, I felt more secure about the coming winter. The shelves were used almost exclusively for food. Either jars with the canned food was there or, after we had eaten the food, we stored the empty jars there. We washed the jars, all were glass, before we stored them down there and before we used them for canning. At first, I thought it was a waste of time to wash the clean jars, but I gradually understood why they had to be cleaned again. If spiders or dirt happened to get in them while they waited, empty on the shelves, they would need to be washed! Who wants to find a dead spider in their food?

When Mom canned peaches she wanted to add some sweetener, but sugar was rationed. To make her own sweetener, because it was not rationed, she used hard, rock candy. The candy was put into a pan of water and boiled until the candy dissolved, and its color too. She didn't use much in each quart, but it did make a difference. Why sugar could be used to make candy, but not so much for home use, in a mystery I never understood.

We also canned green beans, corn, plums and pumpkin. One quart of pumpkin would make three pies. We didn't can pumpkin every year, but once in a while. It took a lot of effort to peal the rind off the pumpkin and clean out the seeds. We grew the pumpkins, that was the easy part.

We did not grow the plums. Mom would buy them by the bushel nearly every year. They were cheap and "healthy." They ensured regularity. As a child, I was not impressed. I began to appreciate that later.

The pits of the plumbs were easy to extract from the fruit. Oftentimes, plums were all we had to eat for the entire meal. Sometimes we also ate them for dessert. The plums were like a mushy sauce after being canned.

We put them on a slice of bread, poured cream over the top and called it dessert. We ate plums so often I can't stand them to this day.

When corn was in season, we would have a meal of corn, but corn was never dessert.

Like all jobs in that house, canning was never a pleasant prospect. I was, naturally expected to do more work than anyone else, though there were parts of the process Mom didn't trust me to do. I was thankful for that. I did a lot of the work of preparing the fruit or vegetables to be canned. And, I could never do it right. The kitchen was hot and steamy. We had no fan or air conditioner. I just endured. The only satisfaction was knowing we would have food to eat in winter.

4-H Experience

When I was ten I joined 4-H. My older sister had been heavily involved in 4-H and I wanted to be too. It was the center of her social life.

All 4-H members had projects to work on. I chose clothing not, any animal or cooking projects, simply because I needed clothes. I had watched my older sister make her own clothes, I wanted to do that too. I needed clothes and thought I could have some choice if I made my own.

I didn't know it then, but 4-H, at that time for country kids, had begun as Corn Clubs for farm boys in Iowa in the early 1900s. In the clubs they learned better ways to grow corn, and other crops, raise dairy cows, and gardening. Girls had their own separate clubs specializing in poultry and gardening. The age limits of 12-18 had dropped by the time I joined.

In 1914, federal funds provided land grant agricultural colleges, in Kansas that was K-State, to extend their work to every county in every state. This was known as the Extension Division of the college. Soon each county office was called simply, the "Extension Office." With the funding came a state-wide position to coordinate 4-H clubs around the state. In Kansas there were nearly 3,000 members in hundreds of local clubs.

The symbol of 4-H is a four-leaf clover, sometimes rare to find and therefore special. The club motto: "To make the best better," gives validation to its members while urging them to improvement. The 4-H pledge, and hence the name, utilizes four attributes which begin with the letter H. This pledge is said at the beginning of local club meetings after the pledge of allegiance to the nation's flag. In the pledge club members dedicate: My Head to clearer thinking, My Heart to greater loyalty, My Hands to larger service, My Health to better living, For my club, my community and my country. Then the meeting begins, run by the members themselves who elect officers each year and gain experience in community organization. Adult leaders, the parents, are present, but generally in the back of the room, to assist when questions arise, but the club members make the club's decisions. It's a good experience in civic participation.

Each member is encouraged to have one or more projects involving some activity that is to be accomplished during the year. Records, financial and otherwise, are expected to be kept of progress on the project and these are judged at the county level. This is training for keeping personal, household or business records. Each club attempts to have at least one adult to assist the members in their project area. They have the role of mentors and cheerleaders as well as teachers.

At first, projects revolved around agricultural education. A member would raise a farm animal, or garden crop, and learn agricultural skills at the same time. Members were cautioned not to consider their project animal as a pet, but emotional attachments were often made. At the end of the summer it was expected the animal to be sold to balance the expense of its purchase and feed. That would complete the economic cycle. Often the sale was heartbreaking for the member who had become attached to their animal.

As the twentieth century advanced, the range of projects broadened out from the farm to include such activities as photography, art and other subjects not agriculturally related so the clubs could benefit urban children as well as rural ones.

The club I joined was the one I knew most about, the one which met at my school: Williams 4-H Club. Getting to the club meetings was a challenge that was seldom surmounted. I could not attend the meetings as often as I wanted because Mom refused to take me. She consistently said she was "too tired," and stayed in bed. There was no one else who could take me. My older siblings had left home and Daddy was not available. He might have been milking our cows or taking care of that day's milk, I don't remember now. I just know I could not go.

Even though the meetings were held at my school, which I walked to and from every day, the meetings were at night, and night was not a time for walking along dark country roads. So, my participation, like many other things, was frustrated. My younger sister, June, was not as interested as I was. She was only eight at the time. If she had wanted as much as I did to attend, would Mom have been more willing to take us? I can't help but wonder about that.

My projects were clothes, not animals, cooking or the garden. I needed clothes and this was a way to have some say in what clothes I had. I managed to make some clothes, with my older sister's help, and every year took several items to the local, county 4-H fair. I learned to sew well. The clothes I took often received ribbons. My mother never commented on them. The prizes weren't as important to me as the fact that I was able to make clothes that I liked and looked good in. I enjoyed sewing and still do. It was magical to me, how small, irregular shaped pieces of fabric, when fitted and attached together in a specific way, magically became a recognizable garment to wear! It is a creative process. I did follow the pattern – that is important. I still create by sewing. Now, I sometimes adjust a pattern in a way that will look more attractive, or even make my own!

One challenge which I succeeded at was a plaid, belted, pleated skirt. My older sister, who taught me, was a perfectionist. Our mother was not. In this case, my sister's insistence on perfection served me well. The plaids had to line up, both at the edge of each pleat and horizontally. This consistency was not easy to obtain and several times I had to take out seams to re-sew them more evenly. I hated the repetition and re-doing work, but when the skirt was finished, all the plaids lined up, even the plaids in the belt. The effect was breath-taking! Stunning!! I still have that sense of accomplishment, though that skirt is long gone.

Her perfectionism, in this case, was a good lesson, though, and, as a result, my seams are straight. Often, people cannot believe I made the clothes I wore – they were so well-done. My dyslexia helped me there: I can visualize a dress, in its pieces, before I sew it up. Yes!

I did participate in other activities of the 4-H club when I was able to attend. I remember one time when Juanita took June and me to sing at the fairgrounds. It was probably for the county 4-H fair. A talent contest was sometimes part of the activities of the fair. Juanita played the piano while June and I sang. The song we chose was, *A Bushel and a Peck.* I don't remember the response, I simply enjoyed the singing. Another time, I had a small part in a Columbus Day pageant my club put on. I was surprised to be included, but the experience helped me feel as if I belonged.

There was one 4-H experience which my mother's non-involvement did not hold me back, and that was a week at 4-H camp. This was held at Rock Springs 4-H Ranch, purchased not too many years before. It was the summer I was eleven. An older couple, whose names I can't remember now, took me and two other kids to the camp south of Junction City. I don't remember the names of the other kids, but they didn't know each other either. They weren't part of my local 4-H club.

On the way, we stopped for a drink. The woman wanted to buy me a Coke. I didn't want one, I wanted water. The woman was frustrated at that, as if I had insulted her. No, I simply preferred water. At home, we didn't often have soft drinks. Mom would sometimes bring home a case of pop, most were orange or grape flavored. Only one was Coke, and that was for her. I wasn't used to drinking Coke and simply wanted water. I didn't know then that soft drinks give only temporary relief from thirst, water is what your body needs – not the sweetener or carbonation. Now, water is in style!

The program and activities at the 4-H camp weren't much different from church camp programs and activities, but that didn't matter. Being there got me away from home – and I didn't have to work! I could be like the other kids: free of responsibilities! One unfortunate thing happened though, trusting young girl that I was. I had a coin purse full of change for buying snacks during the week. One day I left it on my bed. When I went back to get it, it was gone! That was a shocking disappointment, but I survived.

I'm glad I was a part of 4-H but, like so many other things, I wish I could have really been involved. I enjoy being with people and doing things together with others. People energize me.

Being Sick

I remember being sick a lot, sometimes vomiting. One instance stands out. I was in high school. We had no bathroom, so when we were sick we stayed in bed. One time I had vomited over the side of the bed. For some reason no one thought to bring a bucket or any other container, so it all went onto the floor. My mother put newspaper over the mess and let it set. When I was well, she expected me to clean it up. It was my mess. Obediently I did.

I never did this to my children.

Another time, we had gone to a relative's home where I became sick. Not knowing other people went to the bathroom to vomit, I managed to get outside and do it. There was no floor to clean up out there. The relative whose home we were at noticed the mess soon afterwards and asked around to find out who did it. I never confessed. I had no idea what kind of emotional storm, common at my house, would erupt if I did confess. Life was too full of terror anyway.

Dealing with injuries was also different at home then than now. Once, when I was about three years old, I followed my oldest brother when he went to get a bucket of water. He was about eleven. At that age he wasn't too concerned about me. When he had the bucket full of water from the well, he simply headed back to the house leaving me alone. He didn't really want his baby sister following him anyway. The prospect of being alone in that big pasture, so far from the house, scared me, so I hurried to catch up with him.

As he was climbing up the side of the hill to go back to the house I clambered up behind him. He did not know I was hurrying to catch up behind him. In the process I came so close to him that his heel wacked my forehead. It hurt, but that was nothing new, I just wanted to get back to the house with him. When I got to the house, no one noticed the cut. It was hidden by my bangs. We didn't have nightly baths, so the wound was not cleaned or dressed. It wasn't noticed. Eventually it became infected. I don't know what caused it to finally be seen, but fortunately, it was.

Mom could not get the wound clean to stop the infection. It became a major effort that went on for several days. One remedy after another was tried, and nothing worked. I wasn't taken to the doctor, because that was only for life-threatening conditions or broken bones.

Finally Mom tried a new cleaning solution. If it was supposed to clean the house and kill germs, maybe it would clear the infection. In desperation, she dabbed that new cleaning solution on the cut. She diluted it with very hot water before applying it. I remember the pain of the heat, screaming and being held down as she did this. The new stuff killed the germs and the wound finally healed. After that, for cuts in the skin, Clorox was the treatment of choice.

Today, I'm amazed that the scar on the side of my forehead is so minor. It is so minor, I just recently discovered it while writing this story! I'd never thought about it before!! I stopped wearing bangs long, long ago. I don't know if I would have stopped if I'd had a bigger, noticeable scar. I was fortunate and I'm thankful for her action.

The great fear, when I was a child, was polio. At the time no one knew how it was transmitted, only that it was a seasonal, summer epidemic. It was not only debilitating, but deadly; it crippled and killed. This fear lasted until the Sabine vaccine was created. Drops of it were placed in a sugar cube so the sweetness of the sugar would be all you would taste. The sugar cubes were dispensed in small, paper cups. They were the smallest, tiny cups I had ever seen. The cups were as fascinating as the sugar cube, but I never took one home. After the vaccine, the fear of polio became only a memory.

Eventually, it was learned that the polio virus was transmitted due to lack of personal hygiene through water, mostly in swimming pools – which were not as chlorinated then, if at all, as they are now. We couldn't afford to go to any swimming pool, but we were scared to go to places with lots of people, such as the fair, since no one knew how it was transmitted.

Daddy's Stroke

In January of my junior year of high school my brother Don surprised me by coming to get me out of class one day. He told me that Daddy had just had a stroke. It was in his inner ear. The doctor predicted he would never walk again unaided, never drive a car or never work again. My father was determined otherwise.

Within six months he had completely recovered. The doctor was amazed.

Daddy was in the hospital a short time. When he was released he moved in with his sister, Edna, and her husband who lived in Topeka. Coming home to our house would not have been practical since we had no running water or bathroom and he could not move about easily. In Topeka, with those city conveniences, it was easier for him to recuperate.

By summer he had recovered enough to come back home and one day decided to practice driving the car. He was determined to resume functioning. He took the car and drove it in the pasture. When he felt proficient at this he returned to work. His employer, the Santa Fe Railroad, had kept his job open for him. He recovered so completely that people who knew him later had no clue that it had happened. But, I remember the time clearly, it was difficult for the rest of us.

Though his job had been held open for his return, Daddy was only paid for two of the weeks he was out of work. He had no insurance for this kind of emergency. Mom had returned to college to update teaching degree and was now doing her student teaching. There was no income in that. She would eventually return to teaching, but that was months away. There was no financial assistance from anyone. We had no income. In addition, Daddy could no longer do the chores he had done when he was home. I was now stuck with milking the cows and taking care of their milk, in addition to everything else I had done before.

There was not enough food. After returning to college, Mom hadn't put in a garden, it was too much trouble. Now, we were starving. We had a cat we couldn't feed, who had kittens, and they died. I was crushed. I'd always loved baby kittens. Their deaths added to my misery. It was worse because it was winter, the time I hated most.

By now the house was heated with propane gas. It was stored in a tank outside the house. The tank would have to be refilled from time to time as we used the fuel and emptied it. Wouldn't you know it? In the middle of all this – the tank went empty! Now there was no heat!

Our situation was impossible, so one night Mom packed some clothes and we went to stay with Daddy at his sister's for the night. There weren't enough beds in that house so June and I had to sleep on the floor. We sold the cows and chickens then – I don't remember the details and certainly didn't care at the time. We never had cows again.

Ridgecrest

In the summer of 1959 I set out on an adventure where I hoped to reinvent myself away from home. Every summer I had attended church camps, usually in Topeka or Wichita, but that summer I wanted to get further away from home, so for six weeks I attended Ridgecrest, a Baptist camp near Ashville, NC. Instead of being 'Sadie,' I went by my middle name, 'Marie.' I wanted to reinvent myself. I hoped this change would be permanent, but I didn't have the courage to tell my family, so I was back to 'Sadie' when I returned home, but for that one summer I was a new person.

At Ridgecrest, we hiked, attended Bible class, and church services, but the humidity was overwhelming. I caught bronchitis which not only made me miserable, but severely limited my experience there.

My relationship with the other girls was colored by my accent. This was a surprise. Never before had anyone thought I talked funny. The camp was in the south and all the other girls were from the south, so they all sounded "normal" to each other. I did not. I talked different. They would lead me around and asked me to identify different things to see how I pronounced their names. They were entertained by this. I was, again, the outsider, but this time the attention was not malicious. This semblance of popularity was a new experience for me. I wasn't a part of their group, but I wasn't rejected either.

The camp produced a yearbook which every camper received. For a reason I can't remember, if I ever knew, its name was: *Cakira*. It was a typical yearbook with photos, addresses and the school we normally attended. The entry for me read: "Marie Boaz, Waitress, Box 139; Tecumseh, Kansas; Washburn Univ."

All students performed some service during the summer and I worked in the cafeteria. Other positions were: bus boy, hall girl, Nibble Nook (snack bar), crew, kitchen, night watchman, etc. No one looked down on a job a girl did, but I worked during meal times, so wasn't able to eat with the rest of the girls. That major social time was closed to me. Could I have made more friends if I had had that time with them?

At the end of the camp session June came out to see me. The train ride required a transfer at Memphis. When coming to Ridgecrest, Mom had come with me as far as Memphis to make sure I got on the right train there. Now, Daddy came that far with June for the same reason. June and I rode all the way back home together, changing trains on our own. That was fun.

A photograph survived from that summer, from June and Daddy's trip. The time between trains was long enough that they decided to go to the Memphis Zoo. When they arrived at the zoo they learned that that day of the week the zoo was closed to white people. It was the only day of the week black people could go. So she and daddy had their picture taken in front of a sign advertizing the zoo. That was their adventure, and vivid experience of segregation.

Another racial incident happened on that train trip which shocked June so much she had to share with me. Somewhere on the trip by herself, the train passed some black children playing near the train tracks. Being friendly, June waved to them. Another passenger on the train, a white man, scolded her for waving at them. She was stunned. They were little kids, why would it be a crime to wave at little kids? She was learning about The South and its different social expectations. The unfairness remains with her.

Before leaving home for camp, I had seen a piece of fabric in the store that I really, really liked. I asked June to get some of it for me before it was all sold. She did not respond. Her lack of response mystified and upset me. Why couldn't she do a simple thing like that for me when I had done so much for her? I was hurt and bewildered. When she came to visit, she also brought a surprise. She had not only purchased the fabric, but had made an outfit from it for me! I was so amazed and thrilled. Her generosity was so atypical of what I was used to. I'm still impressed. I did, and do, love her, and she showed that she loved me too! You're amazing! Thank you, little sister!!

I wore that skirt and blouse all through college.

My College Career

On Sunday, May 20, 1962, in the college auditorium of Oklahoma College for Woman (OCW) in Chickasha, Oklahoma, now the University of Science and Arts of Oklahoma, I received my bachelor of science degree. The "slow" child finished first!!! WOW!!! My mother didn't comment. She didn't even attend my graduation.

The name of the college was changed three years after I left and, in 2001, the original OCW campus was listed on the National Register of Historic Districts. The school had been founded, under a different name, in 1908 a few years after Oklahoma became a state. The school was commonly called, "OCW." for short. Mine was their fifty-third commencement. Daddy came for this, alone.

Mom, typically, had said she didn't have a dress to wear. Really? I was disappointed, but not surprised.

How could she attend the graduation of her daughter who was not so smart? Attending would validate my intelligence and she could not do that! The fact that I was the first of her five children to graduate college, made no difference.

Three days before graduation, the school had their, "Cap and Gown Day," an occasion for student achievement awards and other ceremonies. The event began with a processional as the graduates entered the college auditorium. As they did this the Glee Club sang, 'God of our Fathers.' Next the sophomores sang, 'Seniors, Seniors.' This was followed by announcements by the current President of Student Government. Next came a scripture reading and prayer by the President of the Interchurch council. Then came messages to the seniors from the Presidents of the freshman, sophomore and junior classes. This was followed by "Faculty Best Wishes," and a response on behalf of the senior class by their President. Individual student achievement awards were presented next and special, "Senior Presentations." Following this, the sophomores sang, "Song of Farewell to the Seniors," the Senior processional, accompanied by 'Auld Lang Syne,' after which the senior class sang a farewell song and the college hymn.

Colleges don't do all of that anymore. Now, it's a curious experience from a former time. For us, then, it was normal, but it didn't interest me that much.

By this time in my life I was married, had stopped school, but had returned to finish when the air force enlistment of my husband was extended from four years to five. It was not his choice. The Cuban Missile Crisis occurred, pushing the world to the brink of nuclear war, and military personnel were retained on high alert.

I had begun college at Washburn University because it was closest to home. She saw a convenience in that. I had wanted to attend Oklahoma Baptist University, but my mother crushed that hope. She insisted I go to Washburn because it was close and I could continue to live at home. I don't know why she hadn't insisted that my older sister attend Washburn, instead she was allowed to go to K-State. I wanted to get away from home, but that was denied. I saw no point in staying home and going to Washburn and eventually flunked out. Would I have succeeded if I had been able to live in town? I don't know, but that was out of the question. I hated having to stay at home. I might as well have still been a little kid! That's what I felt like!

I wondered why I should go to college at all. I was "slow" and not very bright, at least according to my mother who was fond of making pronouncements, on that and anything else. She would constantly sit around and talk about how much money a person would earn if they went to college. I believed her, and enrolled. I didn't know how she thought I would get through college, since I was so slow, couldn't spell and had no idea how to take notes. I was mystified, but that wasn't the worst of it. Living at home, because it cost no more, meant there was only one way to get to class – that was by riding each with my father when he went to and from work in downtown Topeka.

It was embarrassing for me to have to ride my father, in his rickety junker of a truck. We had to leave home in time for him to be at the office 8:00. I would then walk to a bus stop and take a city bus from downtown to Washburn. Most classes were in the morning, so I was finished by early after-noon. I had time to kill until I took the bus back down-town to meet Daddy at 5:00 and ride home with him.

This daily pattern began the summer right after I graduated from Highland Park High School, which was the country high school then. For some reason I never understood, my mother insisted I take biology; to get it out of the way, possibly? I had no interest in biology or Washburn. It was the easiest 'D' I ever earned. No one was surprised. Attending this morning class also meant, to my mother, that it was impossible for me to have any kind of summer job, or any kind of independence. She was in control, and that was the point. This was the rhythm of the short, nearly pointless, first stage of my college career.

Why couldn't I have stood up to her? Defied her? Doing so was inconceivable. I had been so put down and belittled all my life, I had absolutely no confidence in myself. The idea of standing up to her never even occurred to me. I might as well have flapped my arms and flown to the moon. It was impossible.

Later, much later, I realized I could have used the empty time to study, but no one had taught me how to study, certainly not my mother, though she was a teacher. I could have made a secret effort to get an afternoon job, but how could I hide that? I did get a job briefly that year for the Christmas rush, for about two weeks, at Woolworth's drug store, and my mother had a fit. A job was a waste of my time when I could have been studying, she yelled. Then, in retaliation, she and Daddy cut back what little financial support they had given me, so I had less money than before. What was the point of me trying?

In the late fifties women and girls were still bound by social restrictions that had been in place for centuries. My brothers were given more independence than anyone considered for me. Jim, the next oldest above me, had a bicycle, but neither June nor I ever had one. When older brother Don finished high school, he got a job working on a ranch in Oregon. That was fine with our parents. Out oldest brother, Stanley, was drafted into the army. Jim eventually enlisted in the navy. Typical of males at that time, they all had more freedom to leave home than either June or myself. Our older sister had been married for years by this time; that had been her escape.

I did not see any point of continuing the farce of attending Washburn, stopped even pretending to study, and flunked out my second semester. Though it was an act of rebellion on my part, I fulfilled my mother's low expectations for me. But, I could not do the work. When you are constantly and repeatedly told that you can only achieve 'D's, that's what you do.

My mother did not complain about my poor performance, she had been sure it would happen all along. As a consequence, my Washburn career was limited to one summer semester and the next fall and spring semesters. Having done that, I was finally allowed to go to school out of state, which is what I'd wanted to do all along. How bizarre!!

The next fall I went to Oklahoma Baptist University, in Shawnee, Oklahoma, where I majored in Home Ec. While there, I realized that Oklahoma College for Women (OCW), in Chickasha, offered more opportunities, so mid-term I switched. Mom's sister, my Aunt Reba, who had never left Oklahoma, had attended OCW. She was tickled. Our family had another connection, but I don't know the details. My Aunt Reba once told me that my grandfather Yoho had some role in founding of the college. His reputed role remains a curious mystery.

At that time OCW had the peculiar practice of taking any transfer grades as a 'C'. Any grades under that were raised to a 'C', any grades above that were lowered. In my case I had far more lower grades than high ones, so the move paid off. My GPA was bumped up! And I was, finally, free of my parent's constant negativity. Here, at OCW, I was determined to succeed, and I did. I also, from my aunt, had more moral support than ever in my life. That, also, made a tremendous difference!!

Again, at OCW, I tried to have a part-time job. I worked in the cafeteria in the student union serving food. With that job, I was able to have a free lunch. I thought it was a good deal. When my mother found out, she though otherwise. She had her typical fit, cut back what little money I'd been given and insisted I quit.

Eventually my determination, once again, caved in. Even the distance from Kansas could not shield me as much as I had hoped. But there was a ray of light.

Attending college in Oklahoma, I was able to see my Aunt Reba more than while living in Kansas. The college was near where she lived. She was so glad to have another family member close by and we got to know each other much more. Her encouragement and example were critical to my self-esteem and confidence. She made all the difference in my life! She was supportive of me in ways my mother never was. Now, I wish I could have gone to live with her when I was a child. How different my life would have been!!

The impact on young lives which emotional support and encouragement provides is phenomenal and vastly underrated. Knowing my aunt was on my side, my cheering section, so to speak, made all the difference in the world. She was encouraging. I'd never had that before in my life! I'm sure I made mistakes, and could have done many things differently, but she didn't focus on any of that. She was delighted to have one of her nieces close by, she lived only about thirty miles away, and her delight was obvious and infectious. I visited her often.

There was a side benefit to visiting her. I had few clothes so she loaned me some of hers. We were close enough in size that this was possible. I went to her place every weekend – why would I go home? Each weekend, I would borrow some clothes for the next week. We were not the same height, but otherwise the clothes fit.

This expanded my wardrobe considerably. I wonder if the other girls thought I had more clothes than anyone else? I don't know, we never talked about it.

Between my junior and senior years at OCW, I married Walter Rome and became pregnant. This did not deter me from graduating.

My mother's absence from my graduation was not uncommon. She said she didn't have anything to wear, yet she wore nice clothes to teach in every day. Her, "nothing to wear," was a common attitude and response to any event in her children's lives. If she didn't feel like going, she did not. It did not matter how important it was to the child involved. I'm sure this goes back to the absence of a mother in her own life. How could she be supportive, when she had no support? It was a viscous cycle, but when it became my turn to be a mother, I did not follow her example. My children were far happier to be with me, than I ever remember when I was with my mother.

And, I can't help but think that part of her non-attendance of my graduation was from a refusal to admit that maybe I wasn't so "slow," or stupid after all. I had accomplished something of value to her in spite of her beliefs! Though I was the fifth of her children, I was the first of them all to graduate from college. I didn't think much about it at the time, but I couldn't have been so, "slow," after all, if I was **FIRST**! By not going, she did not have to face that fact directly, but she couldn't completely ignore it. In fact, her sister made sure she did not.

A news article about my graduation appeared in the *Marlow Review*, the small town newspaper of Marlow where my Aunt Reba, lived. On Thursday, May 17, 1962 the article appeared. With it was a college photograph of me which I now can't remember having been taken. I didn't know about this news article until years after my mother's death and it was found in the papers my older sister kept, after she, too, had died. I was surprised how good I looked. I don't think I'm photogenic, so this photo surprised me!

The headline read: "**Mrs. Sadie Rome To Receive Degree.**"

Under that was the photograph with the caption: "Mrs. Rome"

Then follow the two paragraphs of the news article: "Mrs. Sadie Rome of Marlow, formerly Sadie Boaz, is among 81 Oklahoma College for Women seniors Chickasha, who are candidates for degrees with the 1962 graduating class. Dr Carles Grady, OCW president, will confer degrees.

"Mrs. Rome is a candidate for a bachelor of science degree in home economics. As an OCW student, she has been a member of Home Economics Club, Baptist Student Union and the Student Education Association. She is the wife of Walter E. Rome, Sussex, N.J. and the daughter of Mr. and Mrs. C. M. Boaz, Tecumseh, Kan."

My Aunt Reba must have supplied the newspaper with the information, I didn't know anything about it – then she must have sent it to my mother to make sure she had a copy. My mother never said a word to me about it. So much for my admiring mother! At least she was consistent.

When it became my turn, I was a very different kind of mother.

Family Reunions

The children of my Boaz grandparent began a family reunion in 1947. It has been held every year since then. Some years well over a hundred people have come, but the numbers are not known for every year. Only the last several decades has there been a sign-in sheet to know who attended. One activity of these reunions is taking family group photos of the families of the original children. These go into the reunion albums, along with the attendance lists.

One summer, when I was in third or fourth grade our neighbor, Mrs. Myers, invited me to attend Vacation Bible School at her church. We had not started going to church so I wanted to go. I didn't know what it might be like, but I liked her, so going anywhere with her was special. And, any time away from home was a good time.

Back then Bible School lasted two weeks. The theme that year was the Ark of the Covenant. One day a teacher came by our class to see if someone would draw the cherub angel to put on top of the Ark of the Covenant. I said I could and I did. I didn't think they thought I could do it, but I did. They said it was good. That Sunday when they had their program I didn't get to go. Daddy's brothers and sisters had decided to start having a family reunion and that Sunday was the first one. I was crushed!

As a child, these reunions were merely something else to be endured, though playing with the other kids was fun. The car ride to wherever they were was not fun! To pass the time, June and I gradually developed a plan. The reunions were always held shortly after school was out. Some time before that we began to save what little money came our way. A nickel was good, a dime was precious, a quarter was a gold mine! With this money, we would sneak to the magazine counter of a store downtown and buy as many comic books as possible. We had to do this in a way our mother would not know, her veto was predictably consistent. We would then save the comic books and force ourselves not to read them. They were for the reunion! On the way to the reunion we would indulge. The seemingly endless hours in the car went quickly while reading. Comic books were generally frowned upon as not being "good" literature, which they weren't, but, oddly, neither of our parents commented on our having them. The comic books kept us quiet, so I guess they were thankful for that!

Only later did I come to appreciate and enjoy those reunions and attended as many as possible and still do. If not for those reunions, I would have had no idea what many members of my extensive family had been doing. Since Daddy was one of eleven children, and several of those children had large families, we are a big family and there is a lot going on!

Theda Vorse, the wife of a cousin, became interested in family history and has become the family historian, tracking as much information as she can of family milestones: births, wedding deaths and other significant accomplishments. Her notebooks are an endless source of fascination, especially for new members of the family. Long ago they filled a table by themselves, now they fill more than one. They have increased in size, and weight over the decades, that now they fill her vehicle – and still she brings food too!

These reunions are held in Kansas, mostly in northeast Kansas where most of us live. It's not uncommon for well over a hundred people to attend. Attempts have been to hold them other places, once as far west as WaKeeney, but less and less attend the further from Topeka they are held. Family members come from all over the U.S. We are scattered. Theda has the details. However, brother Don put all this in his book of family history.

I've brought my children, my grand children, and now my great granddaughter to the reunions. Attending gives them a sense of belonging to something much larger than themselves. Branches of our ancestors have been here since before the Revolution; not only those who immigrated from Europe, but Native Americans as well. We've participated in nearly every major event in American history: wars, the westward migration, homesteading, etc. American history is my family story. And, some family members have given their lives for this country. That is big!

Church

When I was about ten, my aunt Edna started telling Daddy, her little brother, he should be taking his family to church. So, one Sunday we started going to church. He choose a small Southern Baptist church on the west side of Topeka, we lived east of town. Why this church so far away? It was the church his sister, Edna, attended. She was often my Sunday School teacher, but not at first. The first time I walked into the church was the first time I felt love.

"My name is Sadie Boaz," I said when the Sunday School teacher asked my name.

"Do you know that your name is in the Bible?" She asked, in return.

I didn't know that, so she showed me where it was. I was very impressed.

It was not long before I asked Jesus to come into my life and change me. Church became a very important part of my life. I wanted to be there whenever I could. It was a comfort from my home life. No one screamed at me there. We would go on Sunday morning and Sunday night. On the way to church in the evenings we would listen to Jack Benny on the radio. Daddy always took us. Mom stayed home saying she had nothing to wear.

As soon as I learned about summer church camp I wanted to go. I don't know how it was paid for, we couldn't afford it, but amazingly, I was able to go. It was wonderful! Summer church camp was as close to Heaven as I could imagine!

Even though church camp was held in different places, being there wherever it was, was wonderful! It was a time to be away from home and the work I had to do. At camp the staff was nice, no one screamed, I didn't have to do any work, and none of the other kids were mean. There were games and other activities that were fun. The only "work" I had to do at camp was make my bed. That was nothing at all! At home, June and I always wondered if Mom stayed awake at night to think of work for us to do.

I lived all year in anticipation for summer camp. I didn't realize until later, that that was the only time in my childhood that I was able to be a child!

Because we lived so far from church it was hard to get to extra meetings or parties at church that we wanted to attend. Mom would tell me, there would be other times or, my turn was coming. It was a long, long time before that happened. But, it's my turn now and I go to church as often as I can!

Nursery Maid

I love babies. I always have. When my older sister had her first baby, I delighted in taking care of him. This was very fortunate for him, as well as the babies after him. Their mother had no clue how to show her affection. She also had little patience, well… none. She was often overwhelmed. As a result, her response to most adverse circumstances, or anything that didn't immediately go her way, was to rage and scream. Imagine a four year old in an adult body, and you have my older sister. She was not emotionally prepared to be a mother… nor a housewife, or anything else. She simply wanted to do what entertained her at the moment.

This was tragic for her children.

When he was only two and a half, she set Duane, her oldest child, to work, insisting that he give his baby sister her bottle. She didn't want the bother of nursing her. When this second baby could begin to eat some food by herself, my sister decided Duane could help her.

She increased his work load throughout the rest of his childhood. The summer he was thirteen, I convinced his mother to join me to attend summer school far enough away that we had to live there. He was put in charge of the house and his younger two brothers. I thought this would give him a break from his mother. It did. He remembers this as the best summer of his childhood. He was better at this than his mother. But he wasn't the only one she put to work.

Often my sister would call our mother and tell her that she needed help. She "needed" me and June to help. Mom would tell us we had to go. It didn't matter what we wanted, or needed to do otherwise. In the summer time, we often actually lived there, both of us sleeping on the couch, one at each end. This worked until we were old enough there was no room for our feet!

Doing her housework, while she screamed that I wasn't doing it just so to her erratic and exacting expectations, was unendurable, but I enjoyed taking care of the babies. June and I were only eight and twelve when the first baby was born, so we were more like older sisters to the children than distant aunts. That has not changed.

At first, with the first baby, I was at Juanita's by myself and took care of the baby alone. I liked that. I was away from home. I spent a lot of time just holding him. When the second baby came, June also came with me and we each took care of a baby. The third baby was more difficult, we now had to trade off and one child would be left out. When she became pregnant with the fourth, I became resentful. Another baby would mean that much more work for June and myself! Her fifth pregnancy did not come to term, and we were relieved!

One day, when the first baby was not yet two years old, I was pulling him in the wagon outside in the yard and driveway. The driveway was dirt, and after a recent rain, there were ruts that had dried. I was only about thirteen and hadn't thought about the roughness of the dried ruts. As a consequence, the wagon tipped over and Duane spilled out. The tumble naturally startled him and he began to cry.

Being as responsible as I could, I took him into the house to his mother. Crying babies want comfort from their mothers. When we got inside he did not want to go to her, he reached back to me instead. At the time I was pleased. No one had chosen me before, and especially not over a grownup. Only later did I realize how tragic it was for him to know that he would get more comfort from me, a mere child, instead of his mother who should have been his source of comfort. He and I are still close. He helped me with this book.

Eventually, I began to resent and resist my older sister's domineering and dominating ways. She demanded work to be done to her own eccentric standards and never expressed any kind of appreciation or thanks. I began to talk back to her and refuse to meet her demands. I was in high school by this time and entirely fed up with her attitude and actions. Juanita wouldn't stand for this. It wasn't long before she asked only for our youngest sister who had not yet begun to rebel. Then, June was on her own. She continued to be the work horse until she left for a semester of college as an international student in Copenhagen, Denmark. I went out of state to get away, June left the country!

Her children then were, tragically, left alone with their mother. I and June had served as buffers when we were around. Duane escaped as often as he could by slipping out of the house unnoticed and walking nearly half a mile through the pasture to his other grandparent's home. He first did that at two and a half. The other children followed. Mark would get on his bike and ride two miles to the home of friends. But none of them could escape as often as they wanted .

"Who will protect us now?" Was the only question a nephew had for June when she explained why she was leaving. She didn't have the heart to tell him, 'no one.' But that was the truth. He was suicidal within a couple of years and later, in high school, had two mental breakdowns (for lack of a better term). My oldest sister was a worse mother than our own though it's hard to believe that was possible.

These children weren't the only ones I took care of. My brother Don married a widow with three children and together they had one of their own. I took care of them a few times. That was a totally different, and refreshing, experience. My new sister-in-law appreciated my efforts, thanked me, and smiled. That was so different from my own sister. I've liked and respected her ever since!

I've never lost my love for babies and have delighted in my own grandchildren and their children. I think I've passed some of that on because Juanita's children are better parents than she was. June also helped in that. Both of us have stayed active in their lives.

Grandpa Yoho

I had only one grandparent in my life. All the others had died before I was born. The first to die, as I said earlier, was my maternal grandmother, who died in Oklahoma in 1911 when my mother was eight. That was a trauma my mother never recovered from.

My father's parents had died in 1932 and 1935. His family had come to America before the Revolution and one ancestor was in the army at Valley Forge after the hard winter. Three of his sons were in the war of 1812 where one died.

Some branches of my mother's family had come to America in the same colonial decades of this country, others came later. We are a long-time American family.

The only grandparent I knew was Grandpa Yoho, my mother's father. He was the oldest man I knew, so his age is the major memory I have of him. It made him very special, and he lived part time with us.

The Yoho family, like the Boaz, came to America in colonial times and ancestors of both fought in the American side of the revolution. There is still a Yoho castle owned by the branch of the family in Europe.

Johannes and Suzanna Yoho arrived in America in 1738. Their son, Henry, born 1752, enlisted in the revolutionary war effort in 1776 and spent over three years fighting for the new country. Three months of that time he was a spy and, later, spent a year and a half as an Indian scout. The details of his adventures would be interesting, but who knows if anyone wrote them down? It is said that Zane Gray based one of his books on his life. No one remembers which one. Only traces of the bare outlines survive in records. His military service ended when he was wounded in the hip in 1781.

Jumping forward in time, my grandfather, William Harrison Yoho, was born in 1817 in New Martinsville, West Virginia. Grandpa had come to Kansas with his family on the train. He participated in the last land run in Oklahoma. It started around Ponca City, Oklahoma. He staked a claim on 160 acres, but didn't stay on it. He and some other men had come down from Kansas. They didn't want to stay so he went back with them.

One story about his experience said that after the "run" he was waiting at the county courthouse, just a temporary tent with a sign since there were no buildings yet, to register his claim. The line was long and the day was hot. He was approached by a man who offered him a shorter line if he would pay some extra money to him, essentially a bribe. Grandpa was disgusted, and his friends didn't want to wait, so he walked away.

He rode a half Kentucky Thoroughbred in the land run. It was so fast he passed many men riding cow ponies, some even rode wagons. One wagon had a man, his wife and all their children when a wheel came off. Men on horses stopped and put the wheel back on, then went on their way. It was a unique episode in American history.

In his later years, Grandpa lamented his abandoning that land claim, but then he lamented many of his decisions. Few of them were profitable for him.

He met my grandmother in Kansas, but we don't know the details. She was teaching school near Holton, where she grew up, when they met. She quit and followed him to Oklahoma Territory.

"If you're willing, I'm willing," he said to her one day while the two were taking a ride in a buggy. They got married and had two girls. Grandma was the go-getter of the family. Unfortunately, Grandma passed away when my mother was eight years old, her sister was six. The little girls were sick in one bed when Grandma became sick, and then died, in the other. Her father came from Kansas to take her home to be buried.

Life was harder for the three of them after that. Grandpa did not want to leave his girls alone, so he wouldn't consider any job that would make him leave his girls. Instead, he tried to farm. He raised cotton. He never remarried. After attending grade school, Mom took the training to teach school and started teaching. This gave her the only independence she ever knew – and it was short lived. It ended when she married.

Her father eventually became a seasonal Grandpa. The term "snow bird" had not yet been used for summer residency, but that's what he was. He would spend the warm months with us in Kansas and the cold months with Aunt Reba in Oklahoma. There was no consistency in his schedule. When he was at our place he shared a bedroom with my brothers.

A cousin told me that our Grandpa was humorous, but he didn't tell stories or jokes that I remember. I don't even remember his funeral. It was in Oklahoma. My parents attended, I did not. I was just starting high school and felt other things were more important and, by staying home, I had some time without my mother.

Mom

My mother was a beautiful woman. She was born in Oklahoma before it was a state, when it was Indian territory. Her mother kept the family together. She would take the eggs and butter to town to sell. She would often bring a bag of cookies home with her and give the bag to Mom to divide with her younger sister Reba. One day an aunt was there and decided to divide the cookies for the girls. The aunt sat the two piles of cookies on a chair. Mom was so angry at not being able to divide the cookies that she took her hand and swept them all on to the floor. The floor was dirt, the cookies were now inedible.

My mother was severely affected by the death of her mother. My mother was eight. Some have thought she was depressed the rest of her life. They may be right. Not only had Momma died while she was sick, but immediately afterward the rest of her family left her alone with a stranger while they took Momma to Kansas to bury her. My mother was still too sick to travel. I can't image how devastating that double abandonment must have felt to her. And, in those days, there was no one to help with emotional or psychological difficulties. She would surely have benefited from some professional help. If she had gotten help, her whole life, and mine, would certainly have been different! After the death, when my mother was faced with a difficulty, she would go to bed. It was her preferred solution.

After her mother's death, her father expected her to fill some of her mother's responsibilities, such as cooking. Grandpa and the two girls would spend the morning working in the fields, hoeing weeds or something, when Grandpa would send my mother to the house to cook lunch. A while later, when he and the younger daughter would come to the house to eat, they would find no meal, the stove cold and my mother asleep in bed. The responsibility was overwhelming for her at eight years old. That continued to be her solution later in life.

As soon as Mom was old enough she went to school and started teaching school. This was her brief fling with independence. She taught school for seven years and then met my father.

When she was teaching she spent her money on clothes. This must have been compensation for all the years after her mother died and the family was very poor. The dresses she bought were fancy and elegant. Summers, when she wasn't teaching, she didn't get paid, so she would stay with her sister or their aunts. This was typical of teachers of the time. While at her sister's home, and changing clothes, she would take her clothes off and simply drop them on the floor. Her sister was aghast that she would treat such nice clothes so casually, but that didn't matter. She retained this habit of indifference the rest of her life with devastating results for her family.

"Well, you'll probably marry him," her sister commented when Mom told her about meeting Daddy. "Since you're teaching here and he lives there, you won't be around him enough to get tired of him." He lived in Kansas and she lived in Oklahoma.

They eventually had six intelligent and attractive children. However, Mom didn't think so. She categorized us all. Stanley came first and then Juanita. Juanita was Mom's favorite, she considered her beautiful, smart and…perfect.

But family life wasn't easy. She began to feel overwhelmed with two small children, two critical in-laws who lived close enough they could see into her windows, and a husband who expected more attention than she had ever experienced. He was the last baby in his family and his mother was afraid would die as other babies of her had. So he was pampered more than her other children. He had older sisters who treated him as their live baby. He did not want for attention.

His mother was particularly critical of my mother. The two were tied together by the contract Daddy had signed with his parents before he married, stipulating that he would receive the five acres and their two houses after they died, if he took care of them until then. My mother was truly trapped.

After several years of this, she decided to leave Daddy. By this time she knew well that her husband had grown up as the pampered baby of the family. She had had to take care of herself, he could just take care of himself as well! This was a recipe for disaster. I was born into the midst of that disaster.

Mom wanted to take Stanley and Juanita, when they were three and four with her back to Oklahoma where her father and sister lived. Before she could do that, she discovered she was pregnant again. This was more than she could handle. She collapsed and spent much of her time in bed. This left the two little children on their own. Stanley was about four or five and could do some things for himself, such as get dressed and find something to eat. Juanita was eighteen months younger and just learning she couldn't quite dress herself and couldn't find anything to eat. Mom did not get out of bed to help her. She just laid there. Juanita, in her helpless frustration, could not get any help. Her helpless frustration turned to rage. Mom, decades later, told one of Juanita's children, that she was amazed that so much fury could come from someone so little. Juanita

NEVER learned to control her frustration and eventually spewed it all on her own, helpless young children.

When it was near time for the third baby to be born, Aunt Reba came up from Oklahoma to help. The birth went smoothly. Looking at the new baby Aunt Reba remarked that he was cute,

"Yes," Mom retorted. "So's a horse's turd." With that, Aunt Reba stared calling him, "Little H.T." This became too much and Mom finally begged her to stop. His name is Don Allen.

A few years later, when she became pregnant again, Mom didn't tell her sister until after Jim was born. Aunt Reba was outraged. She said she didn't care how many kids Mom had, but she needed to be told in case something happened. With the next baby, something did happen and I was part of it.

In these days, before ultrasound, a woman knew very little about the fetus she was carrying. In my case, there were two of us, but no one had a clue. Unfortunately, my twin didn't make it and Mom almost died too.

Then June was born and I adopted her as my 'twin.' We were together constantly. There was no other girl to play with. And I looked out for her. Our older sister couldn't be bothered. One time, when I was about ten, and June was six, we went shopping. I bought her a dress so she could have something to wear to church. It took all the money I had, and I don't know now how I happened to get that four dollars. I shouldn't have even needed to think about it! That was our mother's responsibility! Not mine.

Mom seldom took us with her when she went shopping. When she did, it was not a rewarding experience, even if it was to get a rare, store-bought dress. She was the one to decide what we would buy and that was that. One summer, in preparation for church camp, she took me shopping. I had hopes for nice, new clothes, but they were dashed. She selected two pairs of shorts. She didn't ask me if I wanted shorts, or liked either one of the pair, she simply made the decision, made sure they fit me and paid for them. I didn't want them. I didn't like them. They weren't like what the other girls were wearing. I never wore them. Someday, I hoped I would be able to choose the clothes that I needed, wanted and liked. The time has finally come when I can do that!

When my eighth grade graduation approached, I needed a dress. Mom took me shopping. We went into the store, of her choice, she pulled a dress off the rack, held up to me for the size and decided to buy it. I had no role in the process whatsoever. I naturally resented that. But now it's my time!

Mom had decided June was the smart one, but not pretty. I was the slow one, but pretty, yet she never let me feel as if I was pretty. Mom worked to make this true. She didn't acknowledge or encourage any achievement of mine and praised June, but not to her directly.

The first time I came home from school with a star on my paper for excellent work, I excitedly showed it to Mom who was working in the garden. She looked at the paper, asking why the star was on it. I excitedly told her of my accomplishment of a perfect score. She simply shrugged and turned back to work. That response was crushing. I felt betrayed. I was betrayed!

I looked more like Mom, while June looked more like Daddy. Did that have anything to do with it? I don't know.

Mom didn't like to cook, but she liked to raise a garden. Her garden always had a row of flowers, always zinnias and others too, but they were mixed right in with the vegetables. When they bloomed she would cut some of the flowers and put them in some water in a fruit jar. Mom didn't see any point in having, or using, a vase. One container of water was as good as another. She didn't think there was anything odd about her actions.

In one of the last years of my mother's life, after I'd been an adult for decades, I went to see her at her home. She was standing outside watching me walk towards her.

"I love you," she said to me. I was so stunned I couldn't respond. It was the first time I'd ever heard those words from her. I wondered what she meant. I still wonder.

Despite her treatment of her children, the cycle of abuse has been broken, either by us or our children.

Over the decades, as I have become older, especially after she died, I've been told that in some ways I resemble my mother in a few mannerisms and posture. I'm not pleased with that, but no longer care. I am my own boss, it's my time!

Genealogy

I was named for my maternal grandmother, Sarah Sadie McAllister, who everyone called 'Sadie.' Few knew her first name was actually Sarah. Hers was a short and tragic life which sent repercussion down several generations. Much of this information has been found through the research and efforts of my brother, Don Boaz, sister, June Clair, and nephew, Duane Herrmann. It has given me a greater appreciation of my place in the family and the history of this country. My family has experienced nearly all of American history. We have been here longer than our country has existed, and the Native branch, much, much longer. One thread has been traced back to England before the Norman conquest in 1066 to the aristocracy. That was a surprise!

The grandmother I am named for became the first school teacher in the family, at least her teaching school is the first that is documented. Members of the next four generations followed her example. Not a bad legacy for one who died at the young age of 33.

But, backing up, her branch, the first McAllisters of my family, John (1817-1907) and Sarah (Miller) (1815-1912), came separately from Ireland, their birth place, in the 1840s to Philadelphia. Both returned home briefly and were married in Londonderry in 1855. His father had been born in Scotland, in the McAllister homeland, but no more has been discovered about him. John and Sarah lived in Philadelphia and may have come as indentured servants. Newspaper items about them say they each worked here seven years before returning home, and that was the normal length of an indenture. John's brother, Adam, had come over also and was the first of the family to live in Kansas. His early death was one of the very first recorded in Calhoun County (first organized by pro-slavery partisans), which is now Jackson County.

John bought Adam's farm and in a few years brought his family out here, partly to remove his son, Sam, from undesirable elements in the big city. Sam's sweetheart had been forbidden to marry him. They were crushed. She married a more acceptable man, had two children, then he died. She was free now and wrote to Sam in Kansas early in 1877. He immediately returned east where they were married. My grandmother was born at the end of that year. A few years later they joined the rest of the McAllister family near Holton.

Sarah Sadie was born 27 December 1877 in Philadelphia and given the name Sarah after her grandmother who had been born in Ireland in 1815. In 1888, when Sadie was ten years old, her mother died. Details of the death are unknown now, but her fraternal mother stepped in to raise the children. The death devastated her father and he never adjusted. He became a vicious drunk to his sons, but spared Sadie the beatings.

My grandmother wanted to escape and be independent and, in 1898, enrolled in the "Normal" training course at Campbell University in Holton. This was a program which trained high school graduates to be school teachers. The name comes from the French term, "Normale," which means 'standard;' a standard course for training teachers. In September that year she is listed as having been hired to teach in Lyons Elementary School in District 86, in Jackson County. The next April the newspaper reported, "Sadie McAllister closed her school in the Lyons district and she gave good satisfaction." (Holton Recorder, 20 April 1899, p.7)

She married William Harrison Yoho, who had been born in New Martinsville, West Virginia. No record was kept of how they met or what brought him to Kansas. It is known that he participated in one of the Oklahoma land runs and staked a claim, but he did not make the claim official.

They settled in Oklahoma Territory and had two girls, my mother was the oldest. They lived in a dirt-floored dugout and, on a trip to the area, my older sister was given directions to a depression on the side of a creek where a dugout had been. The location is now unknown. From the door of the dugout, my mother remembered seeing Native Americans passing by in their traditional dress.

In 1911 the two little girls and their mother, became ill. Mom always said the girls and their mother had different diseases, but the newspaper said they all contracted Typhoid fever. The girls recovered, their mother died. Her father came from Holton and took the body back with him to be buried in the Holton Cemetery with other members of her family.

Aunt Reba had recovered well enough to be taken with her father and grandfather to the burial in Kansas. My mother was still too sick to travel. The obituary reported that she was left with "a trained nurse." To a little girl that would not matter. All she would have known was that she had been deserted by everyone she knew: her momma was dead and her daddy had taken her little sister and left. She never emotionally recovered and mourned the loss of her mother the rest of her life. The depression this loss caused influenced her actions and behavior from then on.

"At least you have a mother," she replied, decades later, in a dead voice to a grandson who pleaded with her to intercede between him and his mother, my oldest sister. He was bewildered with this response. He didn't know what to say. Needless to say, nothing was done. Only later did he remember that her mother had died when she was young and the loss still haunted her.

Daddy's family also came to this country before the revolution and at least one of his ancestors also fought in the war. Abednego, son of Thomas Boaz, was one of the replacement troops after the hard winter at Valley Forge. And, yes, he had two older brothers, Shadrach and Meshach, born in the order they are mentioned in the book of Daniel. There were other siblings as well, but these three names stand out.

Thomas was likely born here but his wife, Eleanor, was born in Ireland. Records are scanty from that time, but they likely married about 1736 and had at least twelve children who survived to adulthood, Abednego was the last.

The tragedy of the Hard Winter was compounded by harsh cold, inadequate food, and an epidemic of smallpox, so as a new recruit, Abednego was subjected to one of the first government mandated inoculations, this one for smallpox. A cut was made in his skin and cowpox pus rubbed in. He became ill, as some did, and could not "muster up" for roll call for three months. When his six month enlistment was over, he was paid only for the three months he was well. He said goodbye to army life and returned to the farm.

Three of Abednego's sons fought in America's next major war, that of 1812. One of these, James, died as a result of wounds received at Fort Mobile. The orders were to, "Hold the fort." He did. His brother, my ancestor, Mignon, bought something from his estate before heading west to the frontier of Indiana Territory. The item was not identified.

The name, Mignon, was most likely inspired by Lafayette's French soldiers who had helped win the earlier war, but there is no evidence the name was pronounced the same way. He had a grandson also named Mignon, but pronounced with a hard G and written evidence indicated the older man also pronounced it that way. He was illiterate most of his life, so others spelled his name and those spellings varied, sometimes even including a Z: "Mizner!"

Mignon wanted to preach, and did so, but he could not read. His wife could, so she read from the Bible and he chose the verses to preach on. He was commissioned to preach by the Baptist Church of Christ at Blue River (which they spelled, "Blew") in 1819. From that date, his life was devoted to preaching the Gospel. He gradually learned to read, even attending school as a grown man, so he could read the Bible himself. He became so renowned for spreading the Gospel in the wilderness that, on his death, a lengthy obituary for him was published in the church magazine. His family is still prominent in that part of Indiana. His wife, Sarah Pope may have descended from the Popes who came to America early in the colonial period, but that is yet to be determined.

Another family link that has not yet been verified is the "connection" to Benjamin Rush, one of the signers or the Declaration of Independence. The Rush family is also large and arrived on these shores shortly after the Mayflower. Mom was always careful to say we were "connected," not that we were descended from, so I think there may be some truth to it.

Mignon and Sarah's second son, Elijah Calloway, was my great grandfather. He was born in Indiana and married Mary Ann Watts who was called Polly. She is reported to be half Indian and would likely have been Miami because that tribe had owned the land there shortly before she was born. This family pushed the frontier westward, homesteading more than once, finally failing to prove a claim in south central Nebraska. Elijah was sixty then. Sometime after that the two separated, she to live with their oldest daughter where she died in Papillion, Nebraska in 1880. He lived with his sister in Iowa, but died years later in Washington state where he is buried in an unmaintained cemetery which has grown back to forest.

He is one of the more colorful characters in my family. His marriage to a Native American, possibly causing the "family problems" mentioned in his father's obituary. Though his father was a minister, he did not marry them. Later in life, Elijah became attracted to the teachings of an itinerant preacher loosely associated with a group of people who eventually organized as the Seventh Day Adventists. Hi is said to have preached their message. They were part of the religious fervor of the mid-nineteenth century. This was evident in America, Europe and Asia. From this time, and this fervor, also came the Church of Jesus Christ of the Latter Day Saints, and Jehovah's Witnesses (in North America), the Templars (in Germany) and the Bábí and Bahá'í Faiths (in Persia). All had some connection to the teachings of William Miller: that Christ would return in the mid 1840s.

In Nebraska, their youngest son, Joseph Martin, my grandfather, met and married Mary Ann Field. They had thirteen children. The Field family had also been in this country since its founding and, also, gradually moved west. They were among the earliest white settlers in Nebraska, where she was born. Her father, Thomas Willis Field, died there, in 1881, much younger than her mother, Armilda Nicholson, who came from a large family active in the affairs of Springfield, NE. She died in Colorado in 1904.

Martin moved his family around, just as his father had done, shown by the various birth places of the children. This may also have been the result of not being much of a success wherever he was or whatever he tried. This, also, was much like his father. Or, it could have been partially due to his temper, which was renowned!

I never knew him, since he died before I was born, but I heard about him, especially his temper. One story told about a neighbor's pumpkins. Grandpa Martin went to a neighbor's farm for some reason when he was angry. He saw pumpkins in a wagon near the neighbor's well. They were ready to be taken to market. In his anger, grandpa threw the pumpkins into the well! This ruined not only the pumpkins, but made the well water unfit to drink! I'm rather glad I never knew him.

Daddy was the youngest child. One baby before him had died and his mother was determined that this baby would live, so he was coddled. This was fine with his several older sisters, who now had a live baby doll to play with and take care of. He learned the world revolved around him. His marriage to my mother, who had had to take care of her own self since the age of eight, was simply a disaster.

His parents could not bear to be separated from him when he went to business school in Topeka, so they followed him. They lived the rest of their lives there and both are buried, in Mt Hope Cemetery. Later, Mom and Daddy were buried next to them, near the tower. Because Daddy went to school in Topeka, got his first (and only) job there, that is where I was born.

Epilogue

I married because that was the normal step for a young woman in the mid 1960s. And, I didn't want to return home after college. I had a teaching degree, but it never occurred to me to live on my own independently. Women's liberation was just around the corner, but I didn't know it. If I had just waited…

My first and second husbands were abusive, which I did not like, but having grown up as an abused child, I didn't know I could expect anything different. I didn't know what I could do about it, but eventually left both marriages. After those learning experiences were behind me, and my children were on their own, I wanted to experience what other people did for a living, so I quit teaching.

Over the years I had discovered that I like talking with people and that most people were friendly, so I looked for a position where talking was required. I also wanted to see more of the country, memories of being stuck on the farm were still with me. I set out on a real journey when I began the next chapter of my life. I was hired by a photography company.

This company sent people all over the country setting up in hotels, churches and other places where people could be photographed and purchase sets of the photos. I explained the prices of the sets and sold the photographs. One day the photographer mentioned that he thought I was dyslexic. I had never heard the word before. He explained it is a condition where the brain changes what the eyes see before processing the information. Sometimes this means, among other things, that words are processed backwards, other times parts of words don't make sense – and people can't spell. That was me!!

In my eagerness to learn more, I discovered the book, *The Gift of Dyslexia*. 'Some gift,' I thought to myself – then I began to read. It all made sense! My struggles in school, my inability to spell – and how this collapsed into other areas of my life. Even something as simple as the difference between right and left is not clear. I had been desperate to know I wasn't stupid, or slow, as I had been so often told – and this book gave evidence that I was not! I was frustrated, and I learned this, too, was typical. Males usually take this frustration out in violence, females turn the violence inward. That's why I allowed myself to be abused. But, the most shattering realization of all was that: MY MOTHER HAD IT ALL WRONG!!!

I had been told that crying was emotionally helpful and even healing, but I had resisted the idea: I'm a grown woman, I'm not going to cry. Nobody's going to make me cry. I have no reason to cry. I won't. But, I did.

The realization that my mother had been so wrong, for so much of my life, unleashed a flood of tears, decades worth of tears. I would cry as I drove from one job to another, I would pull myself together enough to sell the pictures, pack up and set off to the next city, and cry all the way. I basically cried for three months. It was cathartic. The tears washed away the pain and anger and hurt that my mother's words and actions did to me.

She, and the rest of the family, knew nothing about dyslexia. She had not had a sympathetic mother, she had been no mother at all. She had no mother after the age of eight, she did not know how to be a mother. She had no idea how to be supportive of me and my efforts. My life truly had been twisted by the ignorance of those around me, especially my mother. I was now able to forgive her. When the tears were gone, so were the negative emotions of a lifetime. It was such a relief that I became eager to share this discovery with others. That is the reason for this book.

Two of the first people I shared this with were my nephew, Duane, and his son. They didn't know and were struggling. Both are dyslexic with ADD, conditions often found together in males. This nephew, in addition, because of the abuse of his mother, now has PTSD. He, fortunately, learned to read when he was young because of special tutoring one summer suggested by my sister, June. As a result, he has persevered with the writing he has always wanted to do. Now he has several books and stories, poems and articles published in more than a dozen countries around the world, in several languages, and on the internet. In turn, he has helped me with this book.

Dyslexics are intelligent people, often highly intelligent. We are creative and inventive. We are exceptional and that is important!!! For example, I am a good bridge player, I play a mean game of checkers, I can sew better and faster than nearly anyone, I can draw, and successfully create many craft products which I have sold. When I was young, one of the ways I made money was to make corsages out of wood fiber which I sold to ladies of the church. We begin visualizing at an earlier age than the general population. This process of visualization, initially helpful, is untrained and continues in ways that are not helpful. What our eyes see, our brain process as something else. Now I know!

Knowledge is power!

I want to share the revelation of my discovery with others, so I decided to tell my story in hope it will help others understand if they, or someone they know, has problems with reading or spelling, or even as simple thing as knowing where the direction 'left,' as opposed to 'right,' is. My nephew has to figure that out each time – and he's in his mid sixties now. That is merely one of the multiple aspects of dyslexia.

The Gift of Dyslexia, by Ronald D. Davis, explains that dyslexia is manifested uniquely in each affected individual due to that person's individuality. Differences are caused by the talents or predispositions of each person, their environment, including emotional settings, and educational experiences. As a result, no two individuals will have exactly the same symptoms.

The book explains the Developmental Theory of the cause of dyslexia, that very early successful use of visual thinking skills does not transfer from concrete objects to abstract symbols such as letters of the alphabet and words. The stress of trying to apply knowledge of concrete items to abstract symbols makes the learning process more difficult. The child adopts mental tricks in order to appease expectations of their performance by others. Significant loss of self-esteem occurs as learning flounders.

The author explains that multi-dimensional thinking, using all the senses, occurs much faster than verbal thinking. Dyslexics are typically more curious, creative and intuitive than the general population. They are extremely sensitive to their surroundings, are inventive and are good at solving real-world tasks. Once they have experienced something they understand it at a much deeper level and can work with that information on an intuitive level.

The book also provides ways to overcome distorted perceptions and accurately recognize printed symbols, and offers a three dimensional method for doing so. Three reading exercises are offered to improve the ability to read.

By the end of the book the reader can understand the causes of dyslexia and the advantages that come with it and how to function more effectively.

Now you have the knowledge of this experience of one life with undiagnosed dyslexia, you have the power to make a difference. For more information on dyslexia, you can contact: Davis Dyslexia Association International, 1601 Bayshore Ave. Suite 260, Burlingame, CA 94010. Or, see their website: www.dyslexia.com

The Association publishes *The Dyselxic Reader* which contains news of programs developed by the

Association to help dyslexics and those who want to help them, and other related information. Subscriptions are available or individual issues can be purchased. In addition, they also send out a free email bulletin.

Dyslexia doesn't have to stop you. Some well-known dyslexics include: George Washington, Woodrow Wilson, Henry Ford, Thomas Edison, George Patton, Albert Einstein, and many, many others.

I hope you will be able to pass on this information to anyone you know who may seem to have trouble with reading or spelling. They may not know.

Thank you,
Sadie Marie Carpenter

www.ingramcontent.com/pod-product-compliance
Lightning Source LLC
Chambersburg PA
CBHW032133040426
42449CB00005B/228